Old Xiamen

商业老厦门

Cradle of Modern Chinese Business & Chinese Business Education
现代中国商业与工商管理教育的摇篮

〔中英对照 Bilingual〕 | by Dr. Bill Brown
潘维廉 著

厦门大学出版社 国家一级出版社
XIAMEN UNIVERSITY PRESS
全国百佳图书出版单位

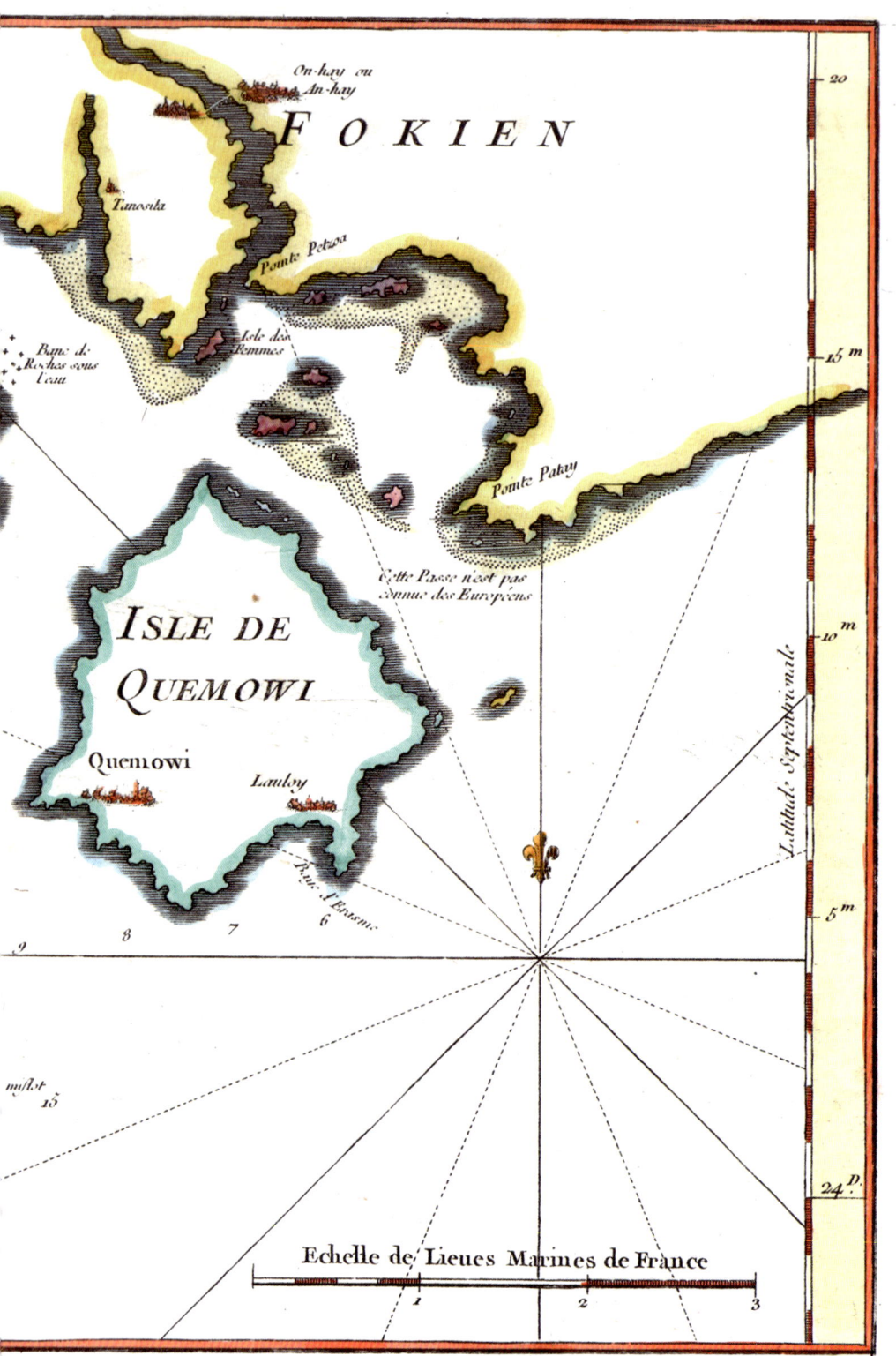

闽南地图，1755年

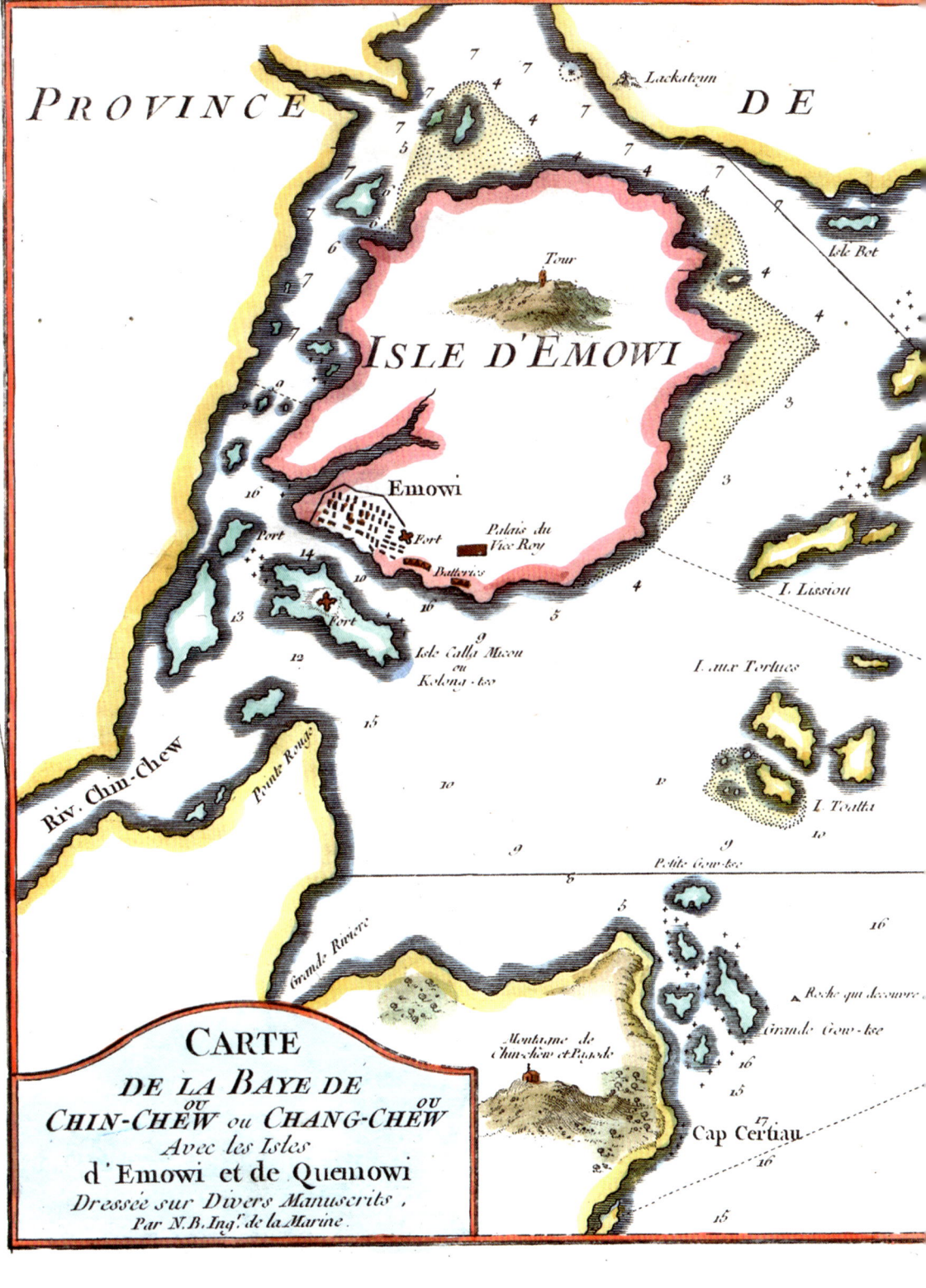

商 业 老 厦 门
——现代中国商业与工商管理教育的摇篮

潘维廉 著

Old Xiamen
(formerly Amoy)

Cradle of Modern Chinese Business & Chinese Business Education

Dr. Bill Brown

of the Jslands of Kulangsoo and Amoy taken from the highest point on Kulangsoo.

Richest Square Mile on the Planet (1920)

"Across a narrow channel—then an hour-and-a-half distant by slow junk [1/4 mile] —lay Kulangsu [Gulangyu], a place of comfortable retirement for the more affluent merchants and at one period a competitor for the reputation of being the "wealthiest square-mile in the world."[①]

Normal Goodall, 1920

"Incidentally it might be stated that there are more wealthy men living on Kulangsu than in any other spot in the world, with the exception of Pasadena, California."

Paul Hutchinson, 1920

"Camel Rock," Bessie Bruce, 1930s

---

① Another foreign writer wrote that in 1920, Gulangyu had more wealthy people than any place on earth, with the possible exception of Pasadena, California. Ironically, I moved here from Pasadena, California.

世界上最富庶的平方英里(1920年)

穿过狭窄的水道,再乘慢船航行一个半小时,就到了鼓浪屿。对比较富足的商人来说,鼓浪屿是一片舒适的乐土。这里还曾经是"全球最富庶平方英里"美誉的竞争者之一。①

——诺缪尔·古德奥,1920年

甚至在1920年,鼓浪屿仍是世界上最富裕的人最多的两个地方之一。

胡金生,1920年

---

① 另外一位外国作者写道,1920年,厦门鼓浪屿是美国加州帕萨迪纳之外全球拥有富裕人家最多的地方。令人啼笑皆非的是,我却从加州帕萨迪纳移居厦门。

Xiamen University, China's Future (1920)

"This school [Xiamen University] is entirely a Chinese institution, with no foreign teachers and no foreign connections, and right out in a small Chinese village. The course of study is being made very practical… When we think of the future days, it is one of the most encouraging things to be seen in the whole of China."

Paul Hutchinson, *A Guide to Important Stations in Eastern China*, 1920

The University of Amoy, The Arts Faculty Buildings looking East. (1920

厦门大学——中国的未来(1920年)

这所学校(厦门大学)是一个名副其实的中国学校,没有外籍教师,没有海外联系,而且地处中国一个小村庄。学科设置实用性很强……想到未来,这是整个中国最激动人心的事情之一。

胡金生:《华东地区主要传教区》,1920年

Old Xiamen
Cradle of Modern Chinese Business & Chinese Business Education

Contents

	Page
Acknowledgements	8
Preface	12
Chapter 1 Ancient Amoy	38
Chapter 2 Why Xiamen Surpassed Canton	58
Chapter 3 China's Most Entrepreneurial People	72
Chapter 4 The Amoy Spirit	92
Chapter 5 Amoy's Peace-Loving Fighters	116
Chapter 6 Gulangyu International Settlement	128
Chapter 7 Xiamen—Cradle of Modern "Chinese" Education	164
Chapter 8 Xiamen University Pioneer in Modern Chinese Business Education	194
Appendix–Some of XMU's Many Firsts	202
Afterward: Two Decades $^+$	220
Bibliography	224

"There is no people in the world wealthier than the Chinese."
        Ibn Battuta   (1304-1358, Arab Traveler who visited Amoy)

Amoy and Gulangyu, 1928 (Bessie Bruce)

目录

鸣谢	9
前言	13
第一章　老厦门	39
第二章　为何厦门胜过广东	59
第三章　中国最富冒险精神的人	73
第四章　厦门精神	93
第五章　热爱和平的厦门斗士	117
第六章　鼓浪屿——外国租界	129
第七章　现代中国教育的摇篮	165
第八章　厦门大学——中国现代工商管理教育的先驱	195
附录　厦门大学之最	202
后记：居厦二十余载	221
参考文献	224

"在这个世界上，没有人比中国人更富有。"
——伊本·贝图塔（威尼斯旅行家，1304-1358）

Acknowledgements

Many thanks to Xiamen University Press (XMUP), and to translator Mr. Pan Wengong of FJTV, who has also translated six of my other books on Xiamen and Fujian.

Warm thanks to Hope College's Amoy Mission Archives, and Mr. Wendell Karsen. Most images from the Amoy Mission are from their collections.

Thanks to Prof. Shen Yifeng, Dean of the School of Management, Xiamen University (SMXMU), for allowing me to use content from our submission for AMBA accreditation. I have been privileged since my arrival in Xiamen in 1988 to witness our fledgling program become the only Forbes and BusinessWeek Top Ten MBA and EMBA programs outside of Beijing and Shanghai—though given Xiamen's rich heritage in both business and education, it should not have come as a big surprise.

Finally, thanks to Amoy's pioneering entrepreneurs, past and present, who built the great Amoy Network of International Trade, and laid the foundation of Xiamen's and SMXMU's success today. These included such men as Xiamen University's founder, Tan Kah Kee [1], the "Henry Ford of Asia," who gave over USD 10 million [2] to education in China and other Asian nations.

---

[1] At one point, Mr. Tan also provided half the funding of Sun Yat-sen's revolutionary Kuomintang Party.

[2] Over 100 million USD in today's dollars.

鸣谢

非常感谢厦门大学出版社和福建电视台潘文功先生——他帮我译校本书以及我之前撰写的其他六本有关福建的书籍。

谢厦门大学管理学院院长沈艺峰教授。承蒙院长准许，本人得以使用学院申报加入英国工商管理硕士协会（AMBA）的认证资料。自1988年来到厦门，我有幸目睹厦大MBA课程从牙牙学语开始，发展成为北京、上海之外唯一列入《福布斯》和《商业周刊》中国MBA及EMBA十佳的院系。当然，以厦门在商业和教育领域拥有的丰富遗产，获得这种荣誉并不足为奇。

最后，我还要感谢厦门历史上和这个时代里富有创新精神的企业家和教育家。他们构建了厦门规模宏大的国际贸易网络，并为厦门及厦门大学管理学院今天的成功奠定了坚实的基础。其中包括被誉为"亚洲的亨利·福特"——厦门大学的创始人陈嘉庚先生[1]。他一生捐献给教育和亚洲其他国家的资金超过1000万美元[2]。

Gulangyu, 1929

---

[1] 陈嘉庚先生曾一度为孙中山先生领导的中国国民党提供了一半的资金。
[2] 相当于现在1亿美元。

Old Xiamen
Cradle of Modern Chinese Business & Chinese Business Education

    Like countless Amoynese before him, Tan was both a visionary and a pragmatist. He started Xiamen University in 1921 with two colleges—the Business College and the Teachers' College—because he knew firsthand that sustainable success in a global business environment, even in his day, required a marriage of both practical business skills and experience with quality education.

Enjoy Amoy!

Dr. Bill Brown
School of Management
Xiamen University

Gulangyu, 1929

商业老厦门
现代中国商业与工商管理教育的摇篮

Tan Kah-kee and Sun Yat-sen

　　与先前无数的厦门人一样，陈嘉庚先生既是一位富有远见的理想主义者，同时也是一名实干家。1921年创办厦门大学时，设立了商学院和教育学院两个学院，因为他从历史的经验中发现，即使在他的那个年代里，要在日益全球化的环境中持续不断地取得成功，也需要把实用的商业技能和经验与高质量的知识教育结合起来。

　　　　　　爱我厦门！

　　　　　　　　　　　　　　潘维廉博士
　　　　　　　　　　　　厦门大学管理学院

Old Xiamen
Cradle of Modern Chinese Business & Chinese Business Education

Preface

One of 3 Richest Places on Earth For its size, it [Gulangyu] is considered one of the three richest places in the world, Pasadena, California being the first. Many wealthy Chinese live here because it is an International Settlement and has protection called extraterritoriality.
  Rose Talman, in Amoy from 1916-1930, unpublished memoirs

The Roaring 20s' Loudest Roar The 1920s were a decade of unprecedented prosperity and optimism, and nowhere did those heady Twenties roar louder than the "wealthiest square mile" on the planet. Gulangyu International Settlement. Only 1/4 of a mile across the bay from Amoy (now Xiamen), Gulangyu was a miniature Hong Kong on steroids. A hotbed of international commerce, cultural exchange, the tiny (1.7 km^2) islet boasted consulates of 14 nations, offices for the world's leading trading firms, and hundreds of elegant mansions thrown up by Amoy's nouveau riche.

Gulangy

商 业 老 厦 门

现代中国商业与工商管理教育的摇篮

前言

全球最富庶的三个地区之一 从规模上来看，它（鼓浪屿）是全球最富庶的三个地区之一。美国加州帕萨迪纳位居第一。许多中国富人在这里居住，因为它是国际租界，拥有被称为"治外法权"的特殊保护。

——摘自罗斯·塔尔曼（1916年至1930年居住在厦门）未出版的自传

20年代最喧嚣的热闹 20世纪20年代，全球经历了前所未有的繁荣与乐观。在令人陶醉的20年代，世界上没有一个地方比全球"最富庶的平方英里"——鼓浪屿国际租界更加喧嚣、热闹。距厦门本岛仅0.25英里，鼓浪屿是香港的微型翻版。作为国际商业、文化交流的温床，这个小岛（1.7平方公里）曾经拥有14个国家的领事馆，全球主要贸易机构的办事处以及数百座由厦门本地新贵兴建的雅致公馆。

(John Otte)

Old Xiamen
Cradle of Modern Chinese Business & Chinese Business Education

Three Generations in Amoy, 1920s-1930s
Bessie Bruce Album (RCA Archives)

Amoy had a greater influence on China's and Asia's development than anywhere else its size, but its power arose not from its stunning wealth but from the unusual people behind it. The International Settlement was an eclectic community of talented and driven foreigners and Chinese who worked together, and used their unique marriage of business prowess and pioneering education to build a foundation that influences Xiamen's business and education even to this day. Of course, Chinese and foreigners had been working together in Amoy for centuries…

商业老厦门
现代中国商业与工商管理教育的摇篮

厦门对中国和亚洲发展的影响要比她的面积大得多。她的影响力并非来自其惊人的财富，而是她身后非同寻常的人民。国际租界是一个由有才干和使命感的洋人和中国人所组成的综合社区。他们一起工作，利用自己杰出的商业才华和创新教育，兼收并蓄，共同为厦门的商业和教育奠定基础，其影响一直延续至今。当然，数百年来，中国人和外国人一直在厦门共同辛勤劳动……

Amoy, 1892 (John Otte)

Old Xiamen
Cradle of Modern Chinese Business & Chinese Business Education

View along the E. Road on Kolong-su.

Gulangyu and Amoy from the Boys' School (about 1892, John Otte)

商业老厦门
现代中国商业与工商管理教育的摇篮

View from the hill to the E. of Typhoon Villa.

On Gulangyu, Looking East (about 1892, John Otte)

Old Xiamen
Cradle of Modern Chinese Business & Chinese Business Education

"The port of Zaytun is one of the largest in the world, or perhaps the very largest. I saw in it about 100 large junks; as for small junks, they could not be counted for multitude."

Ibn Battuta, Arab Traveler (1304-1358)

Centuries before Shanghai and Hong Kong appeared on foreigners' maps of China, Amoy was the "Gateway to South China." With one of the world's deepest natural harbors, Amoy was part of Zayton, the start of the "Maritime Silk Route"—the world's greatest trading port in the Middle Ages, and the object of Columbus' voyages.①

Sinbad's Steps Columbus' sailed West not to discover a New World but a shortcut to an Old World—Zayton, to be specific. He took on his voyage his copy of *Marco Polo's Travels*, in which he had underlined Polo's descriptions of the legendary port rumored to have been frequented by Sinbad himself.②

Section of Moll's Map of China, 1710
Shows "Amoy a British Factory," but no Shanghai or Hong Kong

---

① Fujian Province was the "Birthplace of Chinese Maritime shipbuilding, with oceangoing ships built in the Mawei shipyard 2,200 years ago. By 600 A.D., Fuzhou was already engaged in international trade.

② Many now believe the true Sinbad to have been the Muslim Chinese admiral Zhenghe, who also made 7 epic global voyages, and whose birth name was Sanbao. Even today, temples to Sanbao are found throughout Asia.

商业老厦门
现代中国商业与工商管理教育的摇篮

"刺桐港是世界上最大的港口之一,或许就是最大的!在这里,我看到了大约一百艘大船;至于小船,不可计其数。"
——伊本·贝图塔(1304-1358)

在上海和香港出现在外国人绘制的中国地图上的 数百年之前,厦门就是"通往南中国的门户"。拥有世界上最深的天然港口,厦门当时是刺桐港的一部分,海上丝绸之路的起点。中世纪全球最大的贸易港口和哥伦布远航的目标。①

辛巴达的足迹 哥伦布向西航行,没有发现新世界,却找到通往旧世界——即刺桐的捷径。他在航行中带着《马可·波罗游记》,并标出了游记中马可·波罗对刺桐港的描述。传言称,刺桐港是辛巴达经常进出的港口。②

Amoy, 1927
Jean Nienhuis

---
① 福建省是中国造船业的发祥地。2200年前,马尾的船坞就造出了远洋船舶。至公元600年,福州已经开始从事国际贸易。

② 现在有许多人认为真正的辛巴达就是中国的回教将军郑和,他曾率舰队完成7次史诗般的下西洋航行,其乳名三宝,即使在今天,纪念三宝的庙宇在亚洲仍随处可见。

Old Xiamen
Cradle of Modern Chinese Business & Chinese Business Education

"The Anchor of Amoy, 1845" (Power, 1853)

"And I assure you that for one shipload of pepper that goes to Alexandria or elsewhere, destined for Christendom, there come a hundred such, aye and more too, to this haven of Zayton; for it is one of the greatest havens in the world for commerce."

Marco Polo

The Amoy Network   After the emperor closed the mighty port of Zaiton, China's foreign trade shifted to Canton and Amoy, but Amoy quickly supplanted Canton because of its superior harbor and its more open-minded and entrepreneurial people.

商业老厦门
现代中国商业与工商管理教育的摇篮

"我敢向你保证,假若有一艘船通过亚历山大港进入基督国家的话,就会有100艘、甚至更多的船只进入刺桐港。对贸易界来说,刺桐港是世界上最大的海港之一。"

——马可·波罗

厦门商人圈 当皇帝关闭了刺桐大港后,中国的国际贸易转向广东和厦门,但是厦门很快超越了广东,因为她有条件更优越的港口和思想更开放、性格更进取的百姓。

Amoy Harbor, 1930s　　　　　J. Nienhuis

Xiamenese Outrival Cantonese (1856) "The men of Fokien are, nevertheless, considered to be the boldest and most energetic in China, and when our successes at Canton were talked of, the Chinamen only shrugged their shoulders, and said, "Wait till you go to Fokien; you will pay for it there."
Ball, 1856

Centuries of international trade and broad exposure to world philosophies, religions and academics gave the people of Minnan (South Fujian) a uniquely global outlook. Their openness emboldened them to not only welcome foreigners[①] but also, unlike most Chinese, who are deeply rooted to their ancestral home, to boldly seek their fortunes abroad—largely because they had little choice.

Tough Land, Tough People Fujian is said to be "8 parts mountains, 1 part water, 1 part field." The province is richly blessed with every resource but flat land. The entire province is one range after another—all steep mountains, deep valleys, and raging rivers (which so separated the peoples that today Fujian has more dialects than anywhere else in China). A thousand years ago, the Fujianese engaged in a massive coastal land reclamation program, and over the centuries they terraced their mountains top to bottom for rice and tea, but even so they lacked enough arable land to feed their families. Many Minnan people went into business producing some of China's best silks and porcelains; others became merchants and traders. And countless hundreds of thousands sought their fortune abroad.[②] As a result, most Chinese in other countries were Amoy emigrants or their descendants—which gave Amoynese both at home and abroad a great advantage.

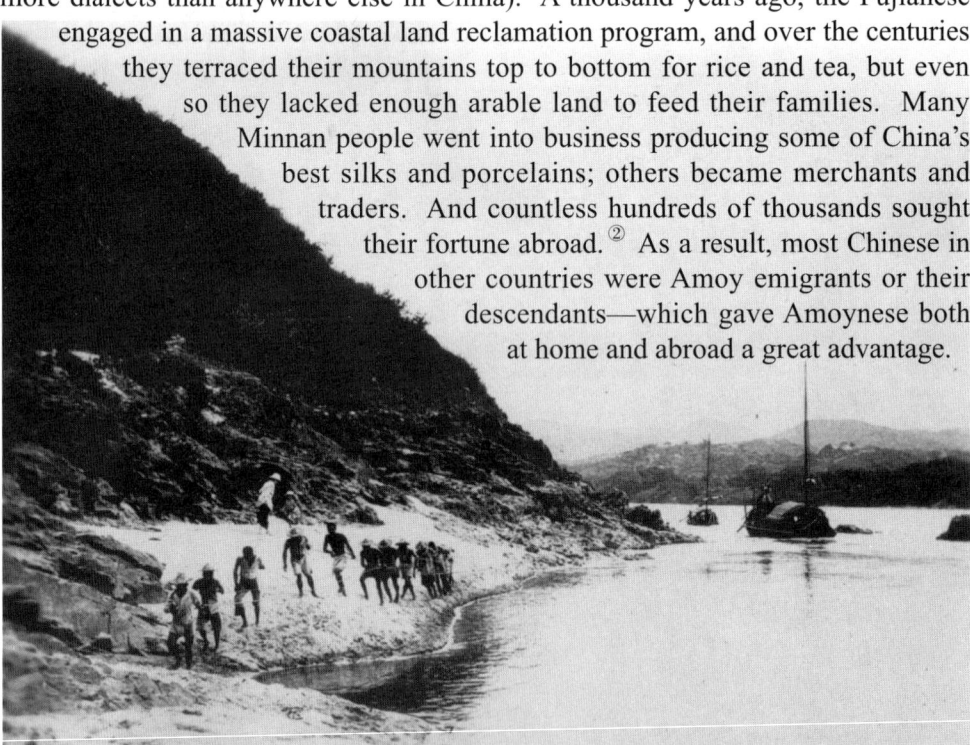

Tracking Upriver, Spring 1932 J. Nienhuis

---

① In Marco Polo's day, our Fujian province even had foreigners holding high-level provincial government posts

② Illegal emigration was punishable by death; I assume that occurred only if they returned.

厦门人胜过广东人（1856年） "不管怎么说，福建人被认为是最大胆、最精力旺盛的中国人。谈及我们在广东所取得的成绩，中国人只是耸了耸肩，说，'等到了福建，你们会为此付出代价的。'"

——波尔，1856年

数百年的国际贸易，以及同世界各国在哲学、宗教和学术等领域的广泛交流，使得闽南人拥有独特的全球视野。厦门人的开放精神反过来促使他们对外国人持欢迎的态度，① 而且跟大多数中国人不同，他们敢于到国外寻找财富。这很大程度上是因为他们别无选择。

艰苦的地方，辛劳的人民　福建素有"八山一水一分田"之称。这个省份资源丰富，独缺平地。全省各地山峦叠起，到处是高山、峡谷和汹涌的河流（它阻隔了人们的交流。至今，福建省比中国其他省份拥有更多的方言）。一千多年前，福建人开始了大规模的围海造地活动。几百年来，他们从山脚到山顶开垦梯田，种植水稻和茶叶。即便如此，他们可用于养家糊口的耕地还是严重不足。因此，他们开始漂洋过海寻找财富。结果，在许多国家，② 大多数的中国人都是厦门移民或其后裔。这给在海外和国内的厦门人带来了极大的好处。

Tough Land, Tough People (Rural Amoy, 1920s)

---

① 在马可·波罗那个时代，福建省甚至有外国人担任政府部门的高官。
② 非法移民当时可判处死刑。我想，这种情况只有在他们归国的时候才会发生。

Old Xiamen
Cradle of Modern Chinese Business & Chinese Business Education

While Amoynese at home gained a reputation as China's best merchants, fishermen, and farmers, their overseas relatives' "Amoy Network"[①] eventually so dominated Asia's trade that other Asians dubbed Overseas Chinese the "Jews of Asia." But far from taking offense, Minnanese abroad were proud to be compared with another displaced people who also survived by their wits, hard work, and high regard for education.

Today, the Chinese in Asian countries, mostly of Minnan descent, are usually only 3 or 4% of the population, yet account for over half of the GDP. And it was their language that eventually brought the world to Amoy's doorstep.

Language Led the World to Amoy   Before the first Opium War (1841) forced treaty ports upon China, most merchants and missionaries sought out Chinese in other Asian countries. Since most of these Chinese spoke the Amoy dialect (also called Minnan, Hokkien), foreigners learned not Mandarin but Amoy.[②] After China opened to trade, these foreigners naturally gravitated to the only place in China where they would not have to learn a new language—Amoy.

Teacher Chhun Hiong Siam-si and some of her pupils, Feb. 1932   J.N.
Teacher Chhun lived to over 100-years-old!
Front: Vandemeer, DePree, VanLinden, Teacher Chen, Renskers, Hofstra, Voskuil
Back: Angus, Holkeboer, Bruce Angus, Holkman, Beekman, M. Poppen, Nienhuis, Dr. Holleman, Veldman, DePree, Platz, Vandermeer, Dr. Hofstra

---

① "Trade and Society: The Amoy Network on the China Coast, 1683-1735," Ng, Chin-Keong, Singapore University Press, 1984

② In compiling this book, I interviewed retired Americans, some over 100-years-old, who had been missionaries and doctors in Amoy during the 1920s to 1950s; they still spoke fluent Amoy, but not a word of Mandarin.

商业老厦门
现代中国商业与工商管理教育的摇篮

坚守故土的厦门人赢得了中国最佳商人、渔民和农民的美誉，而国际"厦门商人圈"①最终主导了亚洲的贸易，因而被其他亚洲人称为"亚洲的犹太人"。对比肩犹太人这个背景离乡的民族，许多闽南商人并不感到被冒犯，而是感到自豪，因为犹太移民依靠自己的智慧、勤劳和对教育的高度重视而生存下来。

如今，在亚洲许多国家，尽管闽南人后裔的人口仅占3%或4%，他们的财富却常常占这些国家GDP的一半以上。正是这些海外厦门人所讲的闽南话把整个世界带到了厦门。

语言把世界带到了厦门　　早在第一次鸦片战争逼迫中国开放通商口岸之前，商人和传教士就开始在亚洲其他国家学习汉语。这些国家的中国人大都来自闽南，讲厦门话（也称闽南话、福建话）。因此，外国人学到的不是普通话，而是厦门话。中国对外通商之后，这些外国人自然而然就聚集到中国的这个地方。②这里讲的是厦门话，他们无须学习一门新的语言。

China's oldest Protestant church, Xinjie, built in 1848 (John Otte, 1900)

---

①　吴振强著：《贸易与社会：中国沿海的厦门网络，1683–1735》，新加坡大学出版社1984年版。

②　为了编辑本书，我曾采访过一些退休的美国人。他们有些已经年过百岁，曾经于20世纪20年代至50年代之间在厦门当过传教士和医生。他们仍然会讲流利的厦门话，但不会说半句普通话。

Old Xiamen
Cradle of Modern Chinese Business & Chinese Business Education

Missions—Education—Business Cosmopolitan Amoynese enthusiastically welcomed and cooperated with foreign merchants and missionaries alike. As a result, Amoy was not only the "Birthplace of Chinese Protestantism," with China's first church, but also had the first medical mission, as well as over 20 pioneering educational institutes that produced some of China's greatest leaders in science, medicine, arts, literature, astronomy, music, sports, etc.

But the relationship between even the open-minded Amoynese and foreigners was often tense, especially as Chinese came to learn, often at gunpoint, that 19th and even 20th century Western trade was often not so much commerce as conquest.

Commerce or Conquest Over the centuries, Amoy entrepreneurs at home and abroad not only survived but thrived, even though their foreign competitors engaged not in free trade but in conquest and control of colonial monopolies, plying the seas with ships like the East India Company's heavily armed 380-ton "Amoy Merchant," which cruised Asian waters from 1681 to 1695.

Chater Collection, 1924

Capture of Amoy, 1840

Manson and Alcock, 1927 — H.M.S. Hornet, Amoy Harbor, 1873

B. Clayton—Piqua

传教——教育——生意 厦门城区的居民热情地欢迎外国商人和传教士,并与他们开展合作。结果,厦门不仅是"中国基督教新教的发祥地"(建起了中国第一座新教教堂),而且拥有中国第一所传教士医院,以及20多个新型教育机构,催生了中国科学、医学、文学、艺术、航空、音乐、体育等领域众多伟大的领导者。

然而,思想开放的厦门人和外国人之间的关系时常紧张,特别是当中国人意识到,枪口之下,19世纪和20世纪的西方贸易经常是征服而非生意。

经商或征战 数百年来,海内外的厦门企业家不仅得以幸存,而且还得到发展,尽管他们所面对的外国竞争者进行的不是自由贸易,而是征服和对殖民地的垄断性控制。外国人出动诸如东印度公司所武装的380吨级"厦门商人号"之类的战船,从1681年至1695年在亚洲海域横行霸道。

Trade or War? "It was during this period [1573-1644] that the Dutch made their appearance by way of Formosa. They took possession of the Pescadores, and landed at Amoy, from whence they penetrated as far as Changchow and Haiting. The Dutch at the time were at war with both the Spanish and Portuguese; their trading-ships went heavily armed, and sailed as much for prizes as for trade."

Denby, 1900

THE ILLUSTRATED L[

ENGLISH OFFICERS DRIL[

商业老厦门
现代中国商业与工商管理教育的摇篮

贸易或大战？ 就在这段时间（1573—1644年），荷兰人借道台湾造访厦门。他们占领澎湖列岛，入侵厦门，并渗透到漳州和海澄等内陆地区。当时，荷兰人正在与西班牙和葡萄牙开战，他们的贸易船只全副武装，四处航行，与其说是为了贸易，倒不如说是为了获取战利品。

——田贝，1900年

N NEWS, OCT. 2, 1875--333

HINESE SOLDIERS AT AMOY.

Old Xiamen
Cradle of Modern Chinese Business & Chinese Business Education

Foreign China Amoynese had no political or military might behind them, even in their own country. While China's foreigners enjoyed extraterritoriality (immunity to Chinese law), Chinese were often subject to foreign law. Foreign nations divided China into "spheres of interests" ① and controlled China's commerce and customs—even setting the amount of tax upon both imports and experts (with, not surprisingly, very low duties on Western imports).

C.A.V. Bowra
Commissioner of Customs
Amoy, 1908

Courtesy of Mike Bass and Jill Fowler

Gulangyu "International" Police
12 Nations' Flags--but not China's

Where is China? "An American pointed at different colored places on a map of China and said his company would work here, or there, or somewhere else, but each time he was told, "No, that belongs to Britain. No, that is French. Can't do—that is Russia's. No, this is Germany's." He finally demanded of the Chinese and European officials, "Where the hell is China!"

La Motte, 1919

---

① In 1899, Lord Charles Beresford published, *The Break-Up of China*, which was essentially a catalogue of China's assets by region, and their benefits for her occupiers.

外国人的中国　即使在自己的国家里，厦门人的背后也没有类似的政治或军事势力。在中国的外国人享受着治外法权（不受中国法律制约），而中国人却时常得遵从外国法律。外国列强把中国划分为多个"势力范围"，并控制了中国的商贸和海关，甚至对中国的进出口贸易设定关税（对西方的进口实行低关税也就不足为奇了）。①

中国在哪里？　"一个美国人指着中国地图上标注不同颜色的地方说，他想在这里、那里或者其他什么地方设立公司。但每一次，他都被告知，'不行，那里属于英国。不行，那是法国人的地盘。行不通，那个地方是俄国人的。不，那个地方是德国人的。'最后，他质问中国和欧洲的政府官员，'中国到底在哪里？！'"

——拉·莫特，1919 年

---

① 1899 年查尔斯·贝雷斯福特勋爵出版《瓜分中国》一书。该书实质上就是中国各地资源的目录及其占领者的利益。

Old Xiamen
Cradle of Modern Chinese Business & Chinese Business Education

Teeth Perish, Tongue Remains   Legend claims that Lao Zi explained the meaning of "Tao" (the "Way") to Confucius by opening his mouth wide but saying nothing. When Confucius' disciples later asked why Lao Zi had not said anything, Confucius replied, "He did! His toothless mouth showed that teeth, which are hard, perish; the tongue, which is soft, remains."

Amoy entrepreneurs' proved the truth of Lao Zi's wordless wisdom. With neither governments nor military at their back, Amoy merchants learned to conduct global commerce on straightforward business principles—much like we teach at SMXMU today.① They discerned the needs of the market and met them, excelling in everything from pineapples, cane sugar, rice milling, rubber and rickshaws to banking, real estate and ocean transport. And in the long run, their "weakness" became their strength.

Bend or Break   Yet another ancient Chinese proverb warns, "Typhoons topple great trees; small, supple trees bend and survive." By the mid 20th century, the tempest of political reform had toppled the great colonial strangleholds upon Asia, and colonial monopolies built not upon commerce but conquest fell with them. Many Chinese business empires, however, grounded on sheer innovativeness and competitiveness, survived.

Rural Amoy, 1920s

---

①   Historians claim Amoy merchants survived because of their Hokkien Network (clan connections, or guanxi), which is true to some extent—but as modern strategy teaches, business success even today depends upon well maintained networks with customers, suppliers, finance, shipping, insurance, etc. Amoy merchants were simply centuries ahead of their time in their mastery of networking.

齿亡舌存　传说老子在向孔子解释"道"的含义时只是张开嘴巴而一言未发。后来，孔子的门徒问，为何老子一言不发。孔子回答说，"他说了！老子张开没有牙齿的嘴巴说的是，'牙齿，无论如何坚硬，都会消失；舌头，即使再柔软，也会幸存'"。

厦门的企业家证明了老子无言的智慧真理。① 背后没有政府和军人撑腰，厦门商人掌握了用直截了当的商业原则进行全球贸易的方法。这些原则至今仍是我们厦门大学管理学院教学的内容。他们洞悉市场需求，并予以满足。从菠萝、蔗糖、稻米加工、橡胶和人力车，到银行、地产和远洋运输，他们样样精通。最终，他们的"弱点"变成了优势。

折弯或折断　曾有一句中国的古训："台风拔大树，小树弯腰存。"到了20世纪中叶，政治变革的暴风骤雨推翻了压在亚洲人民头上的殖民统治，那些依靠征服而非商贸建立起来的殖民垄断也随之坍塌。许多完全建立在创新和竞争力基础上的中国商业帝国却得以幸存。他们利用自己的成功，为他们的居住国和祖籍地厦门谋福利。

1931年迁往大同路的南泰成环球货品大商场营业发达、顾客盈门

---

① 历史学者认为，厦门商人因其福建关系圈（家族联系，或关系）而得以生存。这在某种意义上是真实的。正如现代谋略学所指出的，商业的成功至今仍需依靠与客户、供应商、金融机构、海运和保险公司等维持良好关系。在掌握商业网络方面，厦门商人已经遥遥领先数百年。

Old Xiamen
Cradle of Modern Chinese Business & Chinese Business Education

Investing in the Future   Many early 20th century Western writers praised Amoy entrepreneurs for investing their immense wealth in developing not just their ancestral home of Amoy but their adopted homes as well. Throughout Asia, and in South America, Africa, Australia—wherever they settled and prospered—they built schools, colleges, hospitals, orphanages and social organizations. And they of course invested heavily right here at home, in Xiamen, and Xiamen University…..

Amoy's Army of Lions

"Better an army of sheep led by a lion than an army of lions led by a sheep."
Philip of Macedonia.

"Better than an army of sheep led by a lion is an army of lions led by a lion."
Bill Brown, Xiamen.

Over the past two decades, the "Garden Island" of Xiamen has won numerous national and international awards [①] for its amazing balance of rapid growth and environmental protection. Xiamen has of course been blessed with exceptional leadership, but leaders' visions are stillborn without capable and committed followers to actually implement them. Xiamen, both past and present, has thrived precisely because of its innovative and open-minded people—leaders like Tan Kah Kee and his son-in-law Li Guangqian in the early 20th century, Ms. Cai Shiyue in the late 20th century, and Ms. Yangying in the 21st century.

Books about Tan Kah Kee

[①]   In Stuttgart, Germany, October 2002, the six international judges unanimously awarded Xiamen the gold in the Livcom Awards, the "Oscar of Livable Communities." One judge told me, "Xiamen was not only number one, but number two was far behind." In 2004, Xiamen was the only city in the world to win the U.N.'s Habitat Scroll of Honor Award.

商业老厦门
现代中国商业与工商管理教育的摇篮

投资未来　20世纪初期，多位西方作家称赞厦门企业家把自己所积累的巨额财富投入更多的商业项目，同时也发展了居住国和祖籍地厦门的经济。从亚洲、南美、非洲，到澳大利亚，无论在哪里定居、发展，他们都会兴办学校、医院、孤儿院和其他社会福利机构。当然，他们投资最多的还是在这里——在故乡，在厦门，以及厦门大学……

厦门的狮子军

"一支由狮子率领的绵羊军胜过一支由绵羊领导的狮子军。"
——菲利普（马其顿）

"一支由狮子率领的狮子军胜过一支由狮子领导的绵羊军。"
——潘维廉（厦门）

在过去二十多年里，"海上花园"厦门岛因其能够在经济快速发展与环境保护之间维持美妙的平衡而摘取了无数的国际[①]和国内大奖。当然，厦门一直有幸遇上优秀的领导人，但是领导者的远见如果没

Tan Kah Kee and Mao Zedong

有得到有能力和有奉献精神的追随者的忠实执行也会胎死腹中。无论是过去，还是现在，厦门的繁荣就是因为她拥有思想开放、富有创新精神的人民和领导。例如，20世纪初期的陈嘉庚和他的女婿李光前，20世纪后期的蔡悦诗，以及本世纪的杨英女士（详见最后一章）。

---

① 2002年10月，在德国斯图加特，六名国际评委一致同意授予厦门"国际宜居城市金奖"，即"宜居社区的奥斯卡"。一位评委告诉我，"厦门不仅是第一名，而且第二名与之相距甚远"。2004年，厦门是全球唯一获得联合国人居奖的城市。

Old Xiamen
Cradle of Modern Chinese Business & Chinese Business Education

Tan Kah Kee bronze statne

So Why This Book? I could easily fill a book with just the inspiring stories of our modern pioneer business people [1] and educators, but perhaps the best way to understand modern Xiamen is to view it through the perspective of its rich past. To that end, this book presents Amoy, both the place and the people, through the eyes of foreigners who were here in Xiamen from the mid 1500s to the late 1940s.

Most of the text and images have been excerpted from "Old Gulangyu in Foreigners' Eyes" (XMU Press), which I compiled over the years from foreigners' journals, diaries, letters, articles, and books, as well as hundreds of old photos, paintings, lithographs, etc. I also have used some material from "Xiamen University—Strength of the Nation" (also XMU Press). With a few exceptions, I add no personal comments, as the original sources speak quite eloquently of why Amoy, then and now, is blessed.

---

[1] For some Amoy success stories, visit www.amoymagic.com/success.htm

商业老厦门

现代中国商业与工商管理教育的摇篮

为何编撰本书？ 有关厦门现代先锋商界人士和教育家鼓舞人心的故事,[①] 不费吹灰之力,我就可以编撰一本书。但是,理解现代厦门的最佳方法也许是对其丰富的历史进行观察、展望。因此,本书通过16世纪中期至20世纪40年代在厦门居住的外国人的眼光,展示厦门这个地方及其人民。

本书的文字和图片大都摘选自《老外看老鼓浪屿》(厦门大学出版社出版)。历时数年,从外国人的刊物、日记、信件、文章和书籍,以及数百张老照片、油画和版画中精挑细选,我编撰了《老外看老鼓浪屿》。我也使用了《魅力厦大》(亦由厦门大学出版社出版)的某些资料。除了极个别地方,我未在书中加入任何个人观点,因为在回答为何厦门的过去和现在都是有福之地这问题上,原文显得更有说服力。

[①] 更多厦门人的成功故事,请登录:www.amoymagic.com/success.htm

Chapter 1   Ancient Amoy

Xiamen Harbor, 1759   Hia-men, or the island and port of Amwy, Emoy, or Amoy, is one of the most convenient and safe harbours in all India [Sic] on account of the road which is formed by that island between it and the continent; which is so deep and capacious, that it can receive 1,000 ships of the largest size, which can come as near to land as they please, and ride safe from all winds; on which accounts its commerce hath increased to such a degree, that there is constantly a vast number of Chinese transports that trade from thence to other parts of India; and the emperor keeps there a garrison of 6,000 or 7,000 men, under the command of a Chinese general.

Sale, 1759

THE TOWN OF AMOY FROM KULANGS

第一章 老厦门

Dukes, 1885

厦门港，1759年 厦门，或称厦门港、厦门岛，在整个印度地区（原文如此。从英国人的角度上来看，可能是"英国东印度公司"开展业务地区的统称——译者注）最便捷、安全的港口之一。厦门港与中国大陆地区的交通网络畅通，港口水深、水面宽阔，可容纳上千艘最大型号的轮船，可随意驶近它们想靠近的陆地，并躲避所有的台风天气。因此，这里的贸易已经发展到相当的规模，经常有大量的中国船只从这里出发，与东印度的其他地区开展贸易。中国皇帝在这里驻扎了六七千人的兵力，有一名中国将领统帅。

——西尔，1759年

Old Xiamen
Cradle of Modern Chinese Business & Chinese Business Education

Xiamen Harbor, 1575   The entrance of that port was a fine sight, for besides being so large that a great number of ships could be contained therein, it was very safe, clean and deep; and from the entrance, it is divided into three arms of the sea and so many ships were cruising under sail on each one of them that it was an amazing thing to see….

Father Martin De Rada, July, 1575

Amoy—800 AD?   Both Amoy and Chinchew [Quanzhou] were celebrated even before A. D. 800 as emporia, and their traders were formerly found in the ports of the Archipelago and India, and as far as Persia…Europeans began to trade at Amoy very soon after their appearance in China.

Mayers and Dennys, 1867

Amoy Harbor, 1872

商业老厦门
现代中国商业与工商管理教育的摇篮

Chinese Trading Ship, 1793, by W. Alexander　Chater Collection

1575年的厦门港　厦门港的入口处视野很好，因为港湾宽阔，可容纳大量船只，而且安全、整洁、吃水深。厦门港从入口处就被分为三条航道，每条航道都挤满了数量众多的海船，实在是美不胜收……

——马丁·德·拉达神父，1575年7月

著名的厦门港——公元800年？　厦门和泉州在公元800年前就是著名的商业中心。来自这两个地方的商人首先出现在东南亚群岛和印度的港口，然后远至波斯……欧洲人一在中国露脸，就开始在厦门做生意。

——梅尔斯和丹尼斯，1867年

Old Xiamen
Cradle of Modern Chinese Business & Chinese Business Education

China's Earliest European Sea Trade?   The first commerce carried on by Europeans with China was at a port called Emouy①, in Fokien.

Dobell, "Counselor to Emperor of Russia," 1830

Ptolemy & Xiamen?   Amoy has been one of the conspicuous names in the history of the Chinese Empire. Being one of the natural entrepots of the nation, it was early brought to the notice of foreign Powers. It is quite likely that this is one of the very places that Ptolemy "the celebrated geographer," mentions in his writings concerning places along the coast of China…there are enough undisputed facts to prove that Amoy was known to the traveler and the merchants in the very earliest centuries of the Christian era…

Pitcher, 1893

Amoy Harbor, 1927

---

① Xiamen was not the first port for foreigners, but the fact that many believed it was suggests the high esteem they held for old Amoy.

商业老厦门

现代中国商业与工商管理教育的摇篮

中国最早的对欧洲的海上贸易？ 欧洲人与中国的第一次商贸活动就是在福建一个叫厦门①的港口进行的……

——都贝尔，沙皇顾问，1830年

Amoy, 1853

J. Veldman

托勒密和厦门？ 历史上，厦门曾经是中央帝国一个著名的地标。作为中国的贸易中心之一，厦门港很早就引起了外国势力的注意。在托勒密这位"著名的地理学家"的著述中所提及的中国沿海地名里，厦门港很有可能就是其中的特别地点之一。然而，厦门早在基督纪年早期就为旅行家和商人所熟知。这一事实是无可争辩的……

——毕腓力，1893年

---

① 厦门港不是外国人第一个到达的港口，但是许多人都认为它是的事实说明他们对早期厦门港的尊崇。

THE Saturday Magazine.

No. 677. JANUARY 21st, 1843. { PRICE ONE PENNY.

THE FIVE PORTS OF CHINA OPEN TO BRITISH TRADE.

AMOY, FROM THE ANCHORAGE, SHOWING THE FORTS.

I. AMOY.

IN previous volumes of the *Saturday Magazine* we have given a historical notice of the origin and progress of the British trade in China; of the city and province of Canton; and of the manners and customs of the Chinese in general; thus presenting such interesting details respecting the remarkable inhabitants of this great empire, as the sources of information up to the present eventful period had enabled us to collect.

But our recent contest with the Celestial Empire, and the interest which has now become attached to those portions of China which have been the scene of conflict, or which are thrown open to us by the late treaty, have caused so much inquiry on the subject, and have clothed the accounts of the latest writers with so great a charm, that we proceed to place before our readers a particular notice of the towns most frequently named in connexion with late events; and especially of the five ports now opened to British enterprise and commerce; together with such additional notices of the Chinese character and condition as our increased acquaintance with their country has enabled us to obtain. A clearer idea will be gained of the subject if our readers will refer to a map of China, as they peruse these articles. They will meet with some inaccuracies in most of our maps, when compared with the latest intelligence, yet they will find it advantageous to consult them.

The five ports we shall notice in the following order—
Vol. XXII.

I. AMOY. II. FOO-CHOO. III. NING-PO.
IV. SHANG-HAI. V. CANTON.

Amoy is a celebrated sea-port in the province of Fokien, on the eastern coast of China, and it will be seen by reference to our illustration, that its scenery has somewhat of a picturesque character, although not indicative of great fertility. Amoy is seated on the left side of a bay which deeply indents the country and forms numerous islands. The importance of this place as a British trading post may be estimated by the description of the city given by the Rev. Mr. Gutzlaff.

The city is very extensive, and contains at least two hundred thousand inhabitants. All its streets are narrow, the temples numerous, and a few large houses owned by wealthy merchants. Its excellent harbour has made it from time immemorial one of the greatest emporiums of the empire, and one of the most important markets of Asia. Vessels can sail up close to the houses, load and unload with the greatest facility, have shelter from all winds, and in entering or leaving the port experience no danger of getting ashore. The whole adjacent country being sterile, forced the inhabitants to seek some means of subsistence. Endowed with an enterprising spirit and unwearied in the pursuit of gain, they visited all parts of the Chinese empire, gradually became bold sailors, and settled as merchants all along the coast. Thus they colonized Formosa, which from that period to this has been their granary; visited and settled in the Indian Archipelago, Cochin-China, and Siam. A population constantly overflowing demanded constant resources for their subsistence, and this they found in colonization.

677

商业老厦门
现代中国商业与工商管理教育的摇篮

Old Xiamen
Cradle of Modern Chinese Business & Chinese Business Education

Amoy Dock & 16 Foot Tides   The rise and fall of the tide at Amoy is considerable, and it thus offers peculiar facilities for the construction and use of docks, two of which are now completed and in full employment. The average rise and fall is about 14½ feet but at high tides exceeds 16 feet.

The docks of Amoy are worthy of notice. Vessels of almost any size visiting the port can here obtain everything necessary for repairs &c. The chief establishment is situated on the Amoy side, but a fine dock is in course of construction at Ku-lang-su. The Company's premises afford every facility for repairing and sparring vessels and for cleaning and painting iron and steam ships. Their large granite dock is 286 feet long on the blocks, and at average spring tides can take vessels drawing 16 to 17 feet water. The dock is fitted with a caisson gate and with a centrifugal steam pump of great power ensuring despatch in all states of the tide. For repairs an ample stock is kept on hand of timber, Oregon spars, sheathing copper and yellow metal, and of every description of material required for dock-yard use. The premises comprise an Engineer's workshop, a large Smithy and carpenter's workshops, and the works are superintended by resident Europeans, viz., a shipwright, an engineer, and a blacksmith. Dry godowns have been erected for the reception of vessels' stores &c., when requiring to discharge them.

Mayers & Dennys, 1867

High tide, 22 September 1899   (Cliang Kuan) Native bustom House.

商业老厦门
现代中国商业与工商管理教育的摇篮

厦门码头和16英尺的浪高 厦门港的潮水涨得快,退得也快,需要特别的设备来建设和使用厦门码头,其中两个已经建好并交付使用。潮水涨落的平均高度是14.5英尺,潮水最高的时候浪高会超过16英尺。

厦门码头值得一看。几乎所有尺寸的船只进港后都可以在这里获得诸如维修等方面的必要补给。主码头坐落在厦门本岛一边,正在建设的另一个码头则位于鼓浪屿。码头厂房可以提供所有的设备来维修或者加壁护条,并为铁船和蒸汽轮船提供清洁和油漆服务。用大理石建造的大码头长286英

Amoy, 1920s J.Nienhuis

oy Bund.

尺,平均大潮可以停靠吃水16到17英尺的船只。码头配备了浮坞门和大功率的离心蒸汽泵以确保在各种潮水情况下保持通讯畅通。至于需要维修的船只,仓库里储备了大量的木料、俄勒冈壁护条、铜套、黄铜以及码头需要的任何材料。码头包括工程师车间、锻冶场和木工车间,所有工作由来自欧洲的造船师傅、工程师或铁匠指挥。码头还建造了干燥的货栈,以便接收和保管船上卸下的货物。

——梅尔斯和丹尼斯,1867年

Old Xiamen
Cradle of Modern Chinese Business & Chinese Business Education

Bon Voyage to Siberia Maru, 1938 (Bessie Bruce Album)

商业老厦门
现代中国商业与工商管理教育的摇篮

Siberia Maru, 1928

AMOY ENGINEERING COMPANY, LTD., KULANGSU, AMOY. [See page 827.]
GENERAL VIEW OF WORKS.
THE BOILER SHED. THE TURNING SHOP.
THE FITTING SHOP. MR. J. D. EDWARDS, Managing Director and Superintendent, and his Compradores.

M M M 2

商业老厦门
现代中国商业与工商管理教育的摇篮

THE NEW AMOY DOCK COMPANY, LTD.

THE DRY DOCK.   MACHINE SHOP.   BOILER SHED.   [See page 826.]
CARPENTERS' SHOP.

Old Xiamen
Cradle of Modern Chinese Business & Chinese Business Education

Amoy—Germany's Base in Asia

Amaranth's first port of call was Amoy, a major port north of Hong Kong, which had become the unofficial center of German trade in East Asia.[1] Diederichs and his fellow crewmen worked hard, exchanging the ship's cargo, German industrial goods, for Chinese silk and Amoy's famous tea. Once their work was done, they had a brief opportunity for shore leave before moving on to the next port of call. Amoy offered sights to intrigue any European traveler, including a famous Buddhist shrine and a large but decaying fortress with stone fortifications and obsolete cannon. Although Diederichs was no stranger to the royal monuments of Berlin and Potsdam, the mysterious and novel Chinese architecture and culture impressed him greatly…

Original about 42cm x 55 cm

Das deutsche Geschwade
Nach einer photographischen

Engraving of German ships in Amoy Harbor, fr

---

[1] 28 Nov. 1896, Admiral Eduard Knorr wrote that he supported the "seizure of Amoy at a later time."

商业老厦门
现代中国商业与工商管理教育的摇篮

厦门——德国的亚洲基地 "不凋花号"停靠的第一个港口就是香港北面的大港口厦门,后来成了德国在东亚的非官方贸易中心。① 迪德里希斯和他的船员尽力把船上的货物——德国的工业产品换成了中国的丝绸和厦门的名茶。交换货物后,他们启程前往下一个港口。之前,他们可以请短假参观海滩的风景。厦门的风景很容易吸引欧洲旅游者,其中就有著名的佛教寺庙和一个用石头筑成的堡垒,不过堡垒有些毁坏了,而且堡垒中的大炮也是过时的。

尽管迪德里希斯非常熟悉柏林和波茨坦的皇家纪念碑,中国神秘奇特的建筑风格和文化还是深深吸引了他。

---

① 1896年11月28日,爱德华·诺尔将军写道,他支持"晚些时候再夺取厦门。"

53

German Man of War, Amoy, 1900 (John Otte)

Lying approximately equidistant between Hong Kong and Shanghai, Amoy possessed a good harbor with a spacious anchorage. The port had become the unofficial center of German naval and mercantile operations in Chinese waters in the past twenty years. Twenty years after Luise's visit, when Diedrichs returned to East Asia as commander of the Cruiser Squadron, Amoy topped the navy's list as a prospective site for an official German naval base in China…

Gottschall, 1903

American Gunboat, Amoy, 1900 (John Otte)

商 业 老 厦 门
现代中国商业与工商管理教育的摇篮

French Gunboat, Amoy (1900, John Otte)

厦门港位于香港和上海之间，是个拥有宽阔的锚地的良港。在过去的20年里，厦门变成了德国在中国海域非正式的海军和商务活动中心。路易斯号停靠厦门20年后，迪德里希斯作为巡洋舰中队指挥官回到了东亚，厦门就是德国海军名单上第一个可以成为德国在中国的海军基地备选港口……

——戈斯夏尔，1903年

Amoy Harbor, 1922 — J. Nienhuis

Beautiful Amoy Harbor The appearance of the harbour as it is approached from the sea is one of considerable beauty. The rugged islands, the rocky hills, the blue water, and the pretty island of Kulangsu with its buildings coloured as in a southern European town, combine to make an attractive picture.

Bowra, 1908

Amoy Bund, 1930s (Nurse Jean Nienhuis)

商业老厦门
现代中国商业与工商管理教育的摇篮

美丽的厦门港 从海上看厦门港美景颇为壮观。高低不平的岛屿，岩石裸露的群山，湛蓝色的海水，与充满欧洲南部小镇特色建筑的美丽小岛鼓浪屿一起，构成了一幅迷人的画面。

——博拉，1908 年

Chapter 2 Why Xiamen Surpassed Canton

Xiamen Surpasses Canton, 1843   The island and city of Amoy will succeed to a large share of that trade, which is hourly passing away from Canton forever. The navigation of the Canton river is tedious, and often insecure,--the entrance to the cove of Amoy is short, deep, and unimpeded. Egress is equally inconvenient from the former city, while vessels may wait in the inner harbor of Amoy, under island-shelter, for favorable weather, and sail almost the moment of its return. Besides the natural advantages, all which have more than once been dwelt on in these brief notices of the great empire of the Chinese, our embassies and expeditions have uniformly found a kindlier spirit, a more generous feeling, predominant at Amoy, towards foreigners, and traders, and visitors, than at other parts of China...

Allom and Wright, 1843

Amoy Harbor, 1873 (Thomson)

商业老厦门
现代中国商业与工商管理教育的摇篮

第二章　为何厦门胜过广东

厦门胜过广东，1843年　鼓浪屿和厦门岛将承接中国对外贸易的一大部分，而广东的份额正在日益缩小。在广东（广州珠江）河面上的航行十分艰苦，且很不安全，而进入厦门港的航道短、水深且畅通无阻。对广州来讲，出港也很不方便，而对厦门来说，轮船可在岛屿的庇护下，在港内等待风和日丽的好天气，并且随时可以返航、出港。除了上述优越的自然条件（中国政府反复在简报中述说）外，我们的使领馆官员和探险人员一致认为，跟其他地方相比，厦门大多数市民对外国人、外国商人和外来游客更加友好、大方……

——阿罗穆和莱特，1843年

Old Xiamen
Cradle of Modern Chinese Business & Chinese Business Education

Open Xiamen People, 1854   Amoy… unlike Canton, is quite open to foreigners, who are indeed freely permitted to enter within the walls of all the other towns and cities on the coast, or accessible from it. In visiting Amoy, the first thing that strikes a foreigner coming from the south is the feeling of delight which he experiences in rambling everywhere unmolested. After being forcibly turned back on entering within the gates of the southern metropolis, as has been my experience repeatedly, it is pleasant to revel in the unrestrained luxury of rambling through the streets, and everywhere within and without the walls of Cap-Che, Amoy, Chang-Chow, &c. … The disposition of the people throughout the whole of the province of Fuh-Keen, in which Amoy is situated, is exceedingly favourable…They are candid, open, and friendly in their intercourse with foreigners. Several large and beautiful churches have been built here.

Gillespie, 1854

Country

开放的厦门人，1854 年 跟广东不一样……厦门对外国人相当开放。我们可以完全自由地进出沿海所有城镇。访问厦门时，对一个来自南边的外国人来说，首先印象深刻的是他可以随意走动，没人干扰。这是一种怎样喜悦的心情啊！在南边，我经常被强力驱出城外。在泉州、厦门、漳州等地，我走街窜巷、出入城门，不受限制，实在令人感到高兴。福建省（厦门系其中一地方）全省各地人民的性格都非常友好……他们率直、开放，与外国人交谈友好。这里已经建起了几座漂亮的大教堂。

——吉勒斯俳，1854 年

J. Nienhuis

Old Xiamen
Cradle of Modern Chinese Business & Chinese Business Education

Xiamen—Home of Overseas Chinese April 7th, 1834

Today we got under way. I cannot omit to notice a few more particulars respecting this most celebrated emporium of Fuhkeen, and one of the greatest in Asia. Its harbour is excellent, and accessible to the largest men of war. The natives of this district seem to be born traders and sailors. Their barren country, which furnishes employment for only a few hands, but far more their inclination, prompts them to leave their home, either for Formosa or the principal emporium of the Chinese empire, or the Indian Archipelago, or for the fisheries along their native shores. Wherever they go, they are rarely found in a state of abject poverty; on the contrary, they are often wealthy, and command the trade of whole islands and provinces, as well by their capital as by their superior enterprise and industry.

Strongly attached to their early home, they either return as soon as they have acquired a small property, or they make large remittances. Many of the merchants, settled in the north part of China, return annually with their profits. It is not surprising, therefore, that a large amount of Chinese shipping belongs to Amoy merchants, and that the greater part of capital employed in the coasting trade is their property. Hence this barren tract is one of the richest in China, from the enterprise of the inhabitants. Here is doubtless one of the best harbours for European mercantile enterprise, both for its situation, its wealth, and the stores of all Chinese exports. At an early period the Portuguese traded here; the Dutch followed them; and the Spanish have to this day a nominal right to come hither…

In their dealings, they have a name for honesty above all other Chinese…Solicitous to cultivate friendship with strangers, they have always associated with them freely, whenever beyond the reach of the government. They have been frequently entrusted with high offices, by those foreign states where they have resided as colonists. One of their descendants, as late as the middle of the last century, ascended the throne of Siam.

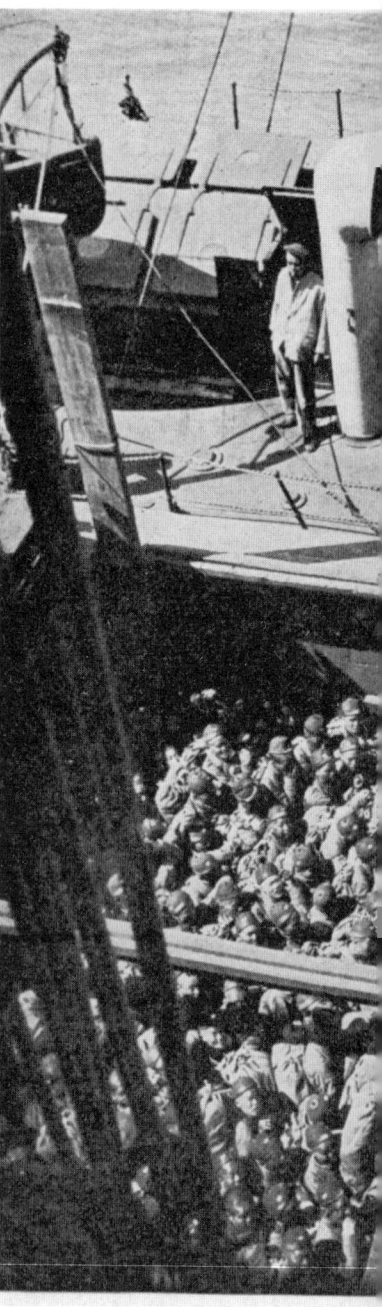

Loa[ding]

Gutzlaff, *Journal of 3 Voyages*, 1834

商 业 老 厦 门

现代中国商业与工商管理教育的摇篮

厦门——华侨的故土　　1834 年 4 月 7 日

今天我们终于启航了。关于福建最著名（同时也是亚洲最伟大的商贸中心之一）的这个商贸中心——厦门，还有几个重要的细节我不能忽略。厦门港是一个深水良港，最大型的战舰能够自由出入。这个地区的人似乎是天生的商人和海员。贫瘠的土地只能容下少量的人口。无奈之余，他们只好背井离乡，要么下南洋，要么去台湾，要么迁居中国主要商业中心，要么就是在沿海打渔谋生。无论他们去哪里，他们很少继续处于赤贫状态。相反，他们很富有。利用手中的资本或优质的企业、生意，他们控制了整个岛屿或全省的贸易。

怀着对故土的无限依恋，他们略有斩获就荣归故里，或向家人大量汇款。许多商人在中国北方做生意，每年都带着钱财回家。因此，厦门商人拥有中国大部分的海运业务和更大份额的沿海贸易资本就不足为奇了。厦门这块贫瘠的土地成了中国最富庶的地方之一，财富主要来自厦门人的生意。无论从地理条件，人民的富裕程度，还是中国商铺的数量，厦门无疑是与欧洲商人开展贸易通商的最佳港口之一。葡萄牙最早到这里做生意，随后而来的是荷兰人，现在西班牙也获得了进入厦门的权利……

生意场上，他们以诚信著名。这一点中国其他地方的人难以望其项背。厦门人很注意发展与生客的友谊，经常自由地与他们交往，不受政府管制。番邦经常授予厦门人殖民地高官，委以重任。上世纪中叶，他们的后代在锡兰王国登基加冕。

——郭施拉：《三次航海日记》，1834 年

63

Old Xiamen
Cradle of Modern Chinese Business & Chinese Business Education

Xiamen Emigration in 1874   Amoy has long been the centre of a large Chinese emigration, and in the year 1874, no less than 16, 500 coolies cleared for Singapore, while a few days after our arrival a large steamer left for the same port with 800 on board. They mostly go to the Malay Peninsula and Dutch Colonies in the Straits of Malacca, and are all from the Amoy district, partly mechanics and partly agriculturists…

…Very many settle down in their adopted countries, but great numbers return home after amassing a competency; some, indeed, after death to be buried near their ancestors, for the Chinese have a deep regard for the mother country, and make a point of having their bodies embalmed, if, that is to say, they can afford it, and being sent back to their native place for burial.

   Shore, 1881

Visionary and Open-mir

商业老厦门
现代中国商业与工商管理教育的摇篮

1874年厦门人下南洋 长期以来，厦门一直是中国大规模对外移民的中心。1874年，16500名苦力离开厦门港，前往新加坡。我们抵达厦门后几天，一艘大型蒸汽船运走了800人，目的地还是新加坡。他们大多数去了马来半岛和荷兰人在马六甲海峡的殖民地。他们都是来自厦门地区，一部分是工匠，一部分是农民。很多人定居在第二故乡，还有不少人在积累相当家当之后返回故土……一些人死后就埋葬在祖先的坟墓旁，因为中国人对故土有深厚的情感。也就是说，如果他们经济上能够承受得起，他们就会想方设法对尸体进行防腐处理，然后运回故乡入葬。

——肖尔，1881年

ynese, May, 1892 (John Otte)

Colonizing but not Conquering   Paradoxical though it may seem to some of our readers, we proceed to state that the Chinese have long been a colonizing people. They have colonized along the sea-board of Asia, from the Sea of Ochotsk to the Bay of Bengal. The Japanese are an offshoot from China. The islands off the coast of China, and many of those in the East Indian Archipelago, have been colonized by the Chinese; and in nearly every kingdom of eastern peninsular Asia they are found in large and influential communities. It is a noticeable fact that whenever the Chinese colonize among a heathen people, their superior civilization gives them at once a decided advantage over the native population.   By their intelligence, industry and capacity for business they almost monopolize all the important and highly remunerative departments of labor; commerce passes into their hands, and they become the chief factors, the leading spirits in the native communities in which they live. ...

Maclay, 1861

Brave Crew of the Famous "Amoy" Junk (sailed from Shanghai to Canada)

Merchant Family　　　　　　　Anderson, 1920

移民，不是占领　　我们常说中国人长期以来一直就是一个对外移民的民族。对于这种说法，一些读者感到有悖常理。事实上，从鄂托斯克海到孟加拉湾，中国人一直沿着亚洲的海岸线迁徙。日本人就是从中国迁移出去的一支旁系。中国外海的岛屿以及东印度群岛（指日本列岛——译者注）都出现过中国人的身影。远古时代，亚洲东部半岛（指朝鲜半岛——译者注）的每个王朝都有影响力极大的中国人大规模聚居区。值得注意的事实是，无论中国人什么时候移居他乡，他们所代表的先进文明赋予他们绝对优越的有利条件，让他们迅速超越本地人。

依靠自己的聪明、勤奋和生意头脑，中国人几乎垄断了所有高回报率的重要工作部门。商业在他们的掌控之中。他们成为居住社区的中坚力量和领导人物……

——麦利和，1861年

Old Xiamen
Cradle of Modern Chinese Business & Chinese Business Education

Foreigners' Description of an Overseas Chinese Industrialist[①], 1930s

[Inspired by the example of Tan Kah Kee]

But perhaps the greatest change in Malayan life is the emergence of the modern Chinese capitalist and industrialist. Singapore has always been famed for its rich towkays. But the towkay of today is a very different being from the courteous, pig-tailed gentleman of two generations back. Externally, at least, he is Westernised from the soles of his brown shoes to his tie and collar, and in the evening he can wear his boiled shirt and dress-coat with the best European. More often than not he wears horn-rimmed glasses.

If he is the son of a rich father, he is almost certain to be a university graduate and perhaps a bencher of one of London's inns of court. If he is self-made and among the Singapore towkays there are still amazing examples of men who began life as an ordinary coolie and became dollar millionaires. He soon acquires the outward attributes of his better-educated compatriots. But in both cases he is a fully-equipped industrialist with the money-sense of a Jew, the gambling instincts of a South African Rand magnate, the modern methods of a Bat'a or a Ford, and the tireless, persevering energy of an old time Glasgow Scot. He runs banks and newspapers.

He has the stock exchange quotations of the world's bourses at his fingertips. He is an authority on commodity prices. He owns rubber estates and tin mines. His factories turn out boots, cheap clothing, food stuffs, including canned pineapples, building materials, medicines, soaps, toys and articles made from rubber, and by the latest methods of modern salesmanship he contrives to export his goods to nearly every country in the world.

Tan Kah Kee's Factory

① Lockhart, R.H. Bruce, *Return to Malaya*, G.P. Putnam & Sons, 1936

外国人对中国海外实业家的描述①（20世纪30年代）

受陈嘉庚事迹的鼓舞

但是，马来人生活最大的变化也许是现代中国资本家和实业家的出现。新加坡一直以其富有的"头家"而著名。但是，现在的头家跟两代之前留着辫子、彬彬有礼的绅士大不一样。至少，从外表上来看，从棕色皮鞋，到领带和衣领，他被西化了。到了晚上，他跟有钱的欧洲人一样穿着熨烫过的衬衫和礼服。他多半还会戴上角质框架的眼镜。

假如他是富家子弟，他几乎肯定是一名大学毕业生，也许是伦敦某个律师学院培养出来的法官。

陈嘉庚，摄于1905年

如果他白手起家，在新加坡头家中，从普通的苦力起家，最终成为百万富翁，类似的惊人事例并不少见。

很快，他获得了其教育良好的同胞的外在特质。但在上述两种案例中，他是一个装备齐全的实业家，拥有犹太人的理财能力、南非兰特财主的赌博天份、巴塔或福特的现代化管理手段以及老派格拉斯哥苏格兰人孜孜不倦、坚韧不拔的能量。他开银行、办报纸。

他对世界各地证券交易所的股票交易行情了如指掌。他是各种商品价格的权威。他拥有多个橡胶园和锡矿。他的工厂生产靴子、便宜的衣物、包括菠萝罐头等食品、建筑材料、药品、肥皂、玩具以及橡胶制品。采用最新的现代推销术，他努力把自己的产品出口到几乎世界每一个国家。

---

① 洛克哈特、R.H. 布鲁斯著：《返回马来亚》，G.P. 普特男父子出版公司1936年版

Outside of his business hours he plays a considerable part in the social life of Singapore, owns houses, takes his wife to the races, and plays golf. He is air-minded, and on the first flight of Imperial Airways from Penang to Hong-Kong the only passenger was a Singapore Chinese called Ong Ee Lim . [1] He is, too, a patriotic citizen and a keen Rotarian, is grateful to the British raj which protects him, and gives valuable service both to the Government Legislative Council and to the various municipal boards of which he may be a member.

Above all, he is a generous giver to local institutions, and like American millionaires is fond of endowing hospitals, colleges and other educational institutions.

He is expatriated, and in some cases is afraid to return to China in her present state. But, although he feels himself at home in the Straits Settlements and is proud of what he has done for Singapore, it would be a mistake to imagine that he has forgotten his homeland…Already some of his profits go to help his struggling country, and there is more than one university, including Amoy, in China that has been founded with Chinese money from Singapore. His services to Malaya have not been forgotten by the British Government, and one of King George's last acts before his death was to confer the first knighthood ever given to a Singapore Chinese on the person of Sir Song Ong Siang, a dignified lawyer, who has devoted the best years of his life to municipal work and to volunteer soldiering in Singapore.

R.H. Bruce Lockhart, 1936

Mr. Tan Kah Kee and Jawaharlal Nehru, India's First Prime Minister

---

[1] The flight from Penang to Hong Kong took two days.

商业老厦门
现代中国商业与工商管理教育的摇篮

工作之余,他在新加坡的社会生活中发挥着相当重要的作用。他拥有房产,带妻子参加赛马,打高尔夫球。他热爱飞行。在大英帝国航空公司从槟榔至香港的首航航班上,唯一的旅客是一名新加坡华人,名叫王益霖。① 他也是一名爱国公民和热心的扶轮社会员,对保护他的英国统治者感恩戴德,为政府立法会和多个市政委员会(他可能是其成员)提供了宝贵的服务。

总之,他是当地慈善机构的热心捐助者。跟美国的百万富翁一样,他也喜欢资助医院、大学和其他教育机构。

他被迫移居国外。就其现状,他在某些情况下不敢返回中国。尽管他安于海峡租界,并为自己对新加坡所作出的贡献感到自豪,但如果说他已经忘记了自己的故乡,那就错了……他盈利的一部分已经被汇回故乡去帮助在困苦中挣扎的国家。在中国,包括厦门,已经不止一所大学,其创办的资金来源于新加坡的华人。

他对马来亚的服务没有被英国政府所忘记。乔治国王去世之前所做的几件事情,其中一件就是首次把爵士称号授予中国人宋旺相。宋是一名尊贵的律师。他把自己一生中最美好的年华献给了市政工作,并在新加坡自愿服役。

——R.H. 布鲁斯·洛克哈特,1936 年

Daonan School, Singapore (One of many financed by Tan Kah Kee)

① 从马来西亚槟榔市至香港的空中飞行要花两天的时间。

Chapter 3 China's Most Entrepreneurial People

Smallest but Richest (1843)   The province of Fokien, in which Amoy is situated, is the smallest of the provinces of China, but is reckoned among the richest, on account of its extensive commerce.

Saturday Magazine, Jan. 21st, 1843

The New Englanders of China   The Fuhkeen (Fujian) men are the New Englanders of China, and their vessels make long voyages, going to all parts of the Chinese coast—to Manila, to Borneo, to Singapore and to Java, but not often venturing as far as India.

Lowrie, 1844

Serie I. No. 4.   Amoy Harbor, about 1900 (John Otte)

第三章　中国最富冒险精神的人

最小，但最富裕　福建省，下辖厦门，是中国最小的省份，但因其规模宏大的商业而被认为是中国最富庶的地方之一。

——《周六杂志》，1843年1月21日

Amoy Junks, 1920s (Bruce)

AMOY.

中国的新英格兰人　福建人堪称中国的新英格兰人。他们驾驶船只远航，足迹遍布中国沿海各地，远至马尼拉、文莱、新加坡和爪哇，有时候甚至到印度探险。

——娄理华，1844年

Old Xiamen
Cradle of Modern Chinese Business & Chinese Business Education

Xiamen Dominates Fujian Trade   The commercial enterprise of the people is to be seen in the fact that Amoy, though possessing only an estimated population of about 150,000, has three times as large a number of trading-junks as the important capital of the province itself. The people emigrate in large numbers to Borneo, Siam, Singapore, Malacca, Batavia, Samarang, and other places in Java; to which parts they resort in the hope of realizing fortunes by commerce, and returning to enjoy the fruits of their industry in their native land.

Smith, 1857

China's Wealthiest Merchants   The district in which this flourishing town is situated, is the most barren in all China, with the exception of Hong-Kong. In spite of these disadvantages, no spot in the empire, numbers so many wealthy and enterprising merchants as Amoy; from whence they have spread themselves all along the coast of China, and have established commercial houses in many parts of the Eastern Archipelago.

Sirr, 1849

One of Dr. John Otte's Wealthy Amoy Patients, about 1905

商业老厦门
现代中国商业与工商管理教育的摇篮

Amoy Harbor MacGowan, 1909

厦门主导福建对外贸易 据估计，厦门人口大约只有 15 万，却拥有了三倍于福建省会的贸易船只。他们的商业冒险精神由此可见一斑。厦门人大量移居文莱、锡兰、新加坡、马六甲、巴达维亚、三宝垄和爪哇的其他地区。他们客居他乡，希望有朝一日能够通过生意积累财富，然后荣归故里、享受荣华。

——四美，1857 年

中国最富有的商人 这座繁荣的小镇所在的区域是中国（香港除外）最贫瘠的地方。尽管条件不好，这个帝国没有一个地方比厦门拥有更多的富商。他们都很有魄力。从这里出发，他们足迹遍布中国沿海各地，并在南洋群岛的许多地方建立了商业机构。

——瑟尔，1849 年

Old Xiamen
Cradle of Modern Chinese Business & Chinese Business Education

Amoynese' Integrity   Over the centuries, Fujianese developed a reputation not only for business prowess but also for unimpeachable integrity. In 1912, Reverend Pitcher wrote in, "I*n and About Amoy*":

> "...what shall we say of them [Fujianese]? They are a part of a wonderful people...
>
> "One hears all kinds of comment upon the deceptiveness of the Chinese and yet in business circles, the commercial world, they have the reputation of being the most straightforward and conscientious merchants in the whole Eastern hemisphere. This holds true here in Amoy...You may always depend upon the man with whom you may be dealing to deliver the goods. No matter how much they may lose in the transaction the Chinese have the reputation of fulfilling their contracts every time to the letter."

Dragon Head (Longtou) Rd., Gulangyu, 1942 (John Anderson)

商业老厦门
现代中国商业与工商管理教育的摇篮

Amoy, Late 1920s (Bruce)

厦门人的诚信　　数百年来,福建人不仅在经商能力方面获得了声誉,诚信方面也是无懈可击的。1912年,皮彻牧师在《厦门内外》一书中写道:

……我们应该怎么评价他们(福建人)呢?他们是一个伟大民族的一部分……

你也许听说过关于中国人不可靠的各种传言。但是,在实业界,在商界,他们拥有东半球最正直、最尽责商人的名声。在厦门也是这样的……你完全可以信任给你送货的生意人。交易中,无论亏掉多少,中国人每次都会不折不扣地履行合同。

Business with Integrity   There are honest merchants and tradesmen of high integrity. It was well known that, during the whole time that trade was carried on with China by the East India Company, there never was an instance of their losing money by the fraud or failure of a Chinese merchant; large sums of money were given to the Chinese by the Company for the purchase of tea in the interior of the country, where they were not allowed to go-often with nothing more than a verbal engagement-with perfect confidence on the one side, and with perfect fidelity on the other. Even if an individual or house of business failed, the family or friends would make up the loss.

Johnston, 1898

An Amoy Gate, 1920s   J. Nienhuis

商业老厦门
现代中国商业与工商管理教育的摇篮

诚实经商 中国人是高度诚信的诚实商人。众所周知,在东印度公司与中国进行贸易的整个过程中,没有发生过因中国商人欺诈、失信而造成亏本的情况。公司向中国商人支付大笔资金,请他们在公司未获许进入的内地代购茶叶,通常只有口头协议。但是,一方信心十足,另一方诚信有加。即便商业机构或某个商人生意失败,整个家族或朋友会先替他弥补损失。

——约翰斯坦,1898 年

Old Xiamen
Cradle of Modern Chinese Business & Chinese Business Education

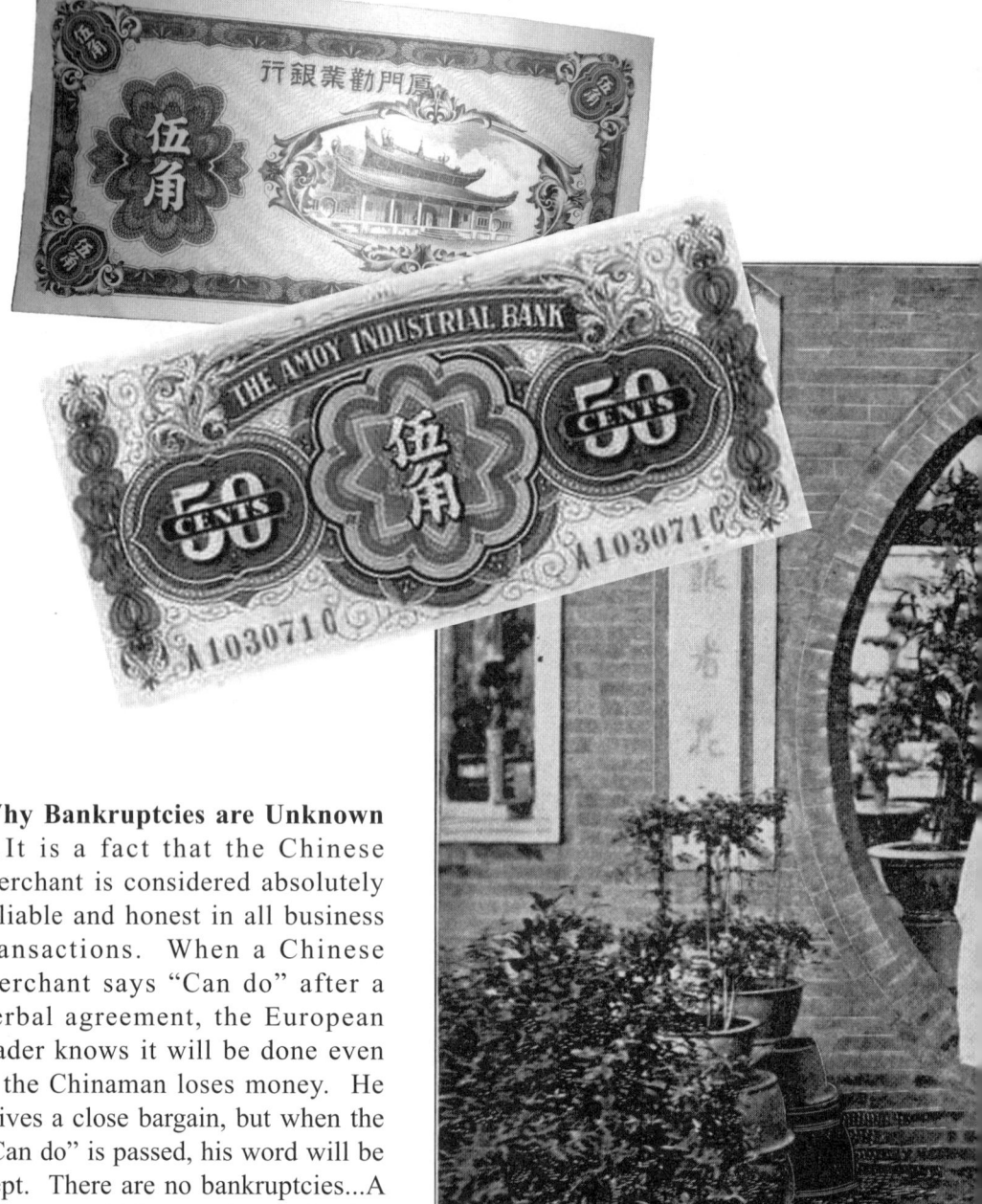

Why Bankruptcies are Unknown
...It is a fact that the Chinese merchant is considered absolutely reliable and honest in all business transactions. When a Chinese merchant says "Can do" after a verbal agreement, the European trader knows it will be done even if the Chinaman loses money. He drives a close bargain, but when the "Can do" is passed, his word will be kept. There are no bankruptcies...A failure would be a serious calamity, for the entire family would be held liable and probably heads would fall.
                                    Caldwell, 1906

为何不知破产　事实是，在所有的商业交易中，中国人被视为完全可靠和诚实的。当中国商人与你达成口头协议之后说，"能做"，欧洲商人知道，生意肯定成了，哪怕中国商人赔钱。中国商人讨价还价逼得很紧。不过，"能做"一出口，他们就会信守诺言。没有破产的说法……生意失败可能会造成严重灾难，因为整个家族都会被牵连，也许还会人头落地。

——凯德威尔，1906年

CHINESE MERCHANTS.　　　　　　　　　　　　　　　Stoddard

Individual Industrialists If any one Chinese virtue occurs more widely and to more marked degree than others, it is probably integrity in workmanship…. Whether a potter struggling to perfect a glaze; an ivory carver laboring for years on a screen worth a king's ransom; or a humble housewife stitching shoe soles for her family, the same patient and painstaking attention is given to detail, the same effort poured into producing what will not only serve the immediate pursuit, but will have beauty and durability as well. Satisfaction in work well done seems to be its own reward in China; certainly no other is apparent in this land where labor, even when it becomes creative art—and only the thinnest line exists between Chinese artist and artisans—is the cheapest of all commodities.

This racial characteristic of thoroughness may be due to the Middle Kingdom's having been throughout the centuries a civilization composed of individual industrialists. The largest establishments rarely consisted of more than the proprietor and six or seven helpers; great factories and mills appeared only with the introduction of foreign methods. Any man trained in a craft could set up business for himself in his own home; doing all the work in person or being assisted by the members of his household until that day when he could afford to feed and shelter an apprentice.

Lewis, 1938

Amoy Rickshaws (1930s, Bessie Bruce)

Making Quilts, 1892 (John Otte)

个人手工业者 如果说中国人有一个比别人更显著、更为人所知的优点,那可能就是他们工艺方面的尽善尽美……陶工努力工作,让瓷器的釉面完美,象牙雕刻师可以在价值连城的屏风上用工多年,或者说纯朴的家庭主妇为自己的家人缝补鞋底,再小的细节也给予了同样的耐心和勤勉。他们注入同样的心血,不仅是为补好鞋底,而且还要让鞋子漂亮、耐穿。在中国,对工作完美收官的满意本身似乎就是对自己的奖赏。尽管劳力有时会变成富有创造性的艺术,而且中国艺术家与艺术工匠之间只有细微的差别,但在中国这片土地上,显而易见的,那就是劳力是最便宜的商品。

中国人完全、彻底的民族特性也许可以归究于数百年来中央帝国的文明是由个人手工业者构成的。在最大的商业机构,业主很少雇用超过六、七个帮工;大工厂、大作坊也仅局限于介绍国外的生产方式。受过训练的手艺人一般只在自己的家里营业,自己亲自动手,或者让家里人帮忙,直至他能供得起一个徒弟的食宿。

——列维斯,1938 年

Amoy Workers Too Competitive?
Mr. Gearys chief complaint against the Chinese was that they work too cheaply, are too industrious, and do not eat as much as an American. He obtained his information from Consul Bedloe, of Amoy. He says the average earnings of the Chinese adult employed as mechanic or laborer (in China) is five dollars per month, and states that this is ten per cent above the average wages prevailing throughout China.

"...Is it fair to subject our laborer to a competitor who can measure his wants by an expenditure of six cents a day, and who can live on an income not exceeding five dollars a month?"

Anonymous Letter in Henry Gratton, *As a Chinaman Saw Us*, 1904

Amoy Coolies (1907, MacGowan)

商业老厦门
现代中国商业与工商管理教育的摇篮

Amoy Carpenters, 1892 (John Otte)

厦门工人太有竞争力？ 葛瑞先生对中国人的主要抱怨是他们的工作太廉价，太勤劳，而且不像美国人吃得那么多。他从厦门壁洛领事那里得到了这些资讯。他说，在中国，一个人受雇当技工或辅助工，他的收入是每月5美元，并指出这已经高出中国现行薪资平均水平10%。

让我们的劳工与需求仅为每日开支6美分、靠每月不超过5美元收入就能生活的中国人竞争，这合理吗？

——摘自亨利·格拉顿著《一个中国人眼中的美国人》中的一封匿名信，1904年

Amoy, Jan. 1934　　J. Veldman

Old Xiamen
Cradle of Modern Chinese Business & Chinese Business Education

Lollipop and Toy Maker, 1934   J. Veldman

Open-air Noodle Shop, 1934

Knife and Scissors Sharpener, 1934

Open-air Barber Shop, 1934

商 业 老 厦 门
现代中国商业与工商管理教育的摇篮

Making Sugar, 1892 (John Otte)

Grinding Rice　　MacGowan, 1912

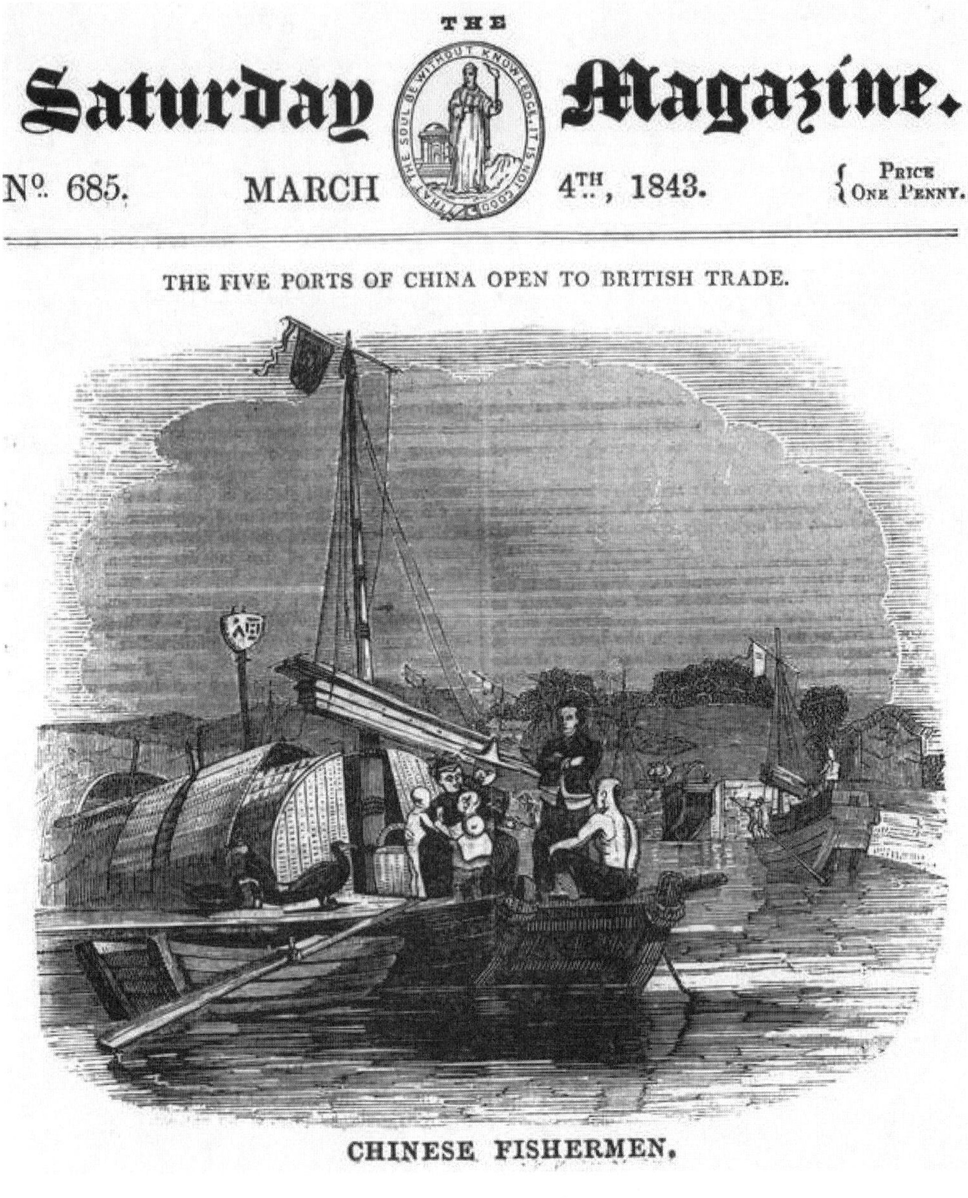

The Saturday Magazine.

Nº. 685. MARCH 4TH, 1843. { PRICE ONE PENNY.

THE FIVE PORTS OF CHINA OPEN TO BRITISH TRADE.

CHINESE FISHERMEN.

China's Most Daring Fishermen   Of all the Chinese fishermen, which is a very numerous class of people, the natives of Fuhkeen [Fujian] are the most enterprising and daring. The greater part of the Chinese coast is visited by them; they brave all dangers for a scanty livelihood, and suffer the severest hardships to return to their families with five dollars after the toils of a whole year.

Gutzlaff, 1834

商 业 老 厦 门
现代中国商业与工商管理教育的摇篮

Longtou Jetty, Gulangyu, 1920s　　　J. Nienhuis

中国最勇敢的渔民　中国的渔民数量庞大。在所有的中国渔民中，福建本地渔民胆子最大，最富有冒险精神。他们到过中国大部分沿海地区。他们冒着各种各样的风险，为的是获得微不足道的生计。他们经历了最艰难的困苦。一年劳累，带回家里的只有五元钱。

——郭施拉，1834 年

Amoy, Early 1930s (Bruce)

Cormorant Fishing, Amoy (1900, John Otte)

89

Old Xiamen
Cradle of Modern Chinese Business & Chinese Business Education

Amoy Farm, 1930s (Bruce)

World's Best Farmers   There are no more clever farmers in the world. Their farms are exceedingly small, compared with American farms. They are kept under a high state of cultivation, and around about Amoy are expected to yield two crops each year.

Their little farms of half an acre to three or four acres, some terraced one above the other up the hillside, have more the appearance of garden spots than otherwise.

Pitcher, 1893

Rural Amoy, 1920s (Bruce)

商 业 老 厦 门
现代中国商业与工商管理教育的摇篮

Threshing, 1922   J. Nienhuis

世界上最棒的农民   世界上没有（比中国农民）更聪明的农民了。与美国农场相比，他们的农田特别得小。农田的耕作水平很高，厦门及其周边地区，农作物一年可收获两次。

    他们的农田从半英亩到三、四英亩，有些农田就修建在山坡上，就是一层叠一层的梯田，外表看上去更像是园艺场。

——毕腓力，1893 年

Amoy Irrigation, 1922   J. Neinhuis

Chapter 4 The Amoy Spirit

Grandpa MacGowan, 1907

Xiamenese' Zest For Life In this, our first year in China, an astonished excitement possessed us. We were confronted by a strange civilization of unparalleled richness. To unfold it was at once alarming, delightful, baffling. It radically altered the nature of my world. It was as if I had opened the smooth familiar back of my watch for the first time and discovered within the complete, complex and inexorable interaction of fine-toothed cogs—a whole self-sufficient system which had been going on all the time, and I unaware of it. It demanded, paradoxically, a jettisoning of preconceived European ideas of China and the Chinese, while requiring the best and highest of Western wisdom and culture as a yard-stick by which to measure and understand its anomalies as well as its heights. In spite of the appalling state of the country… underneath it all was China, solid and enduring…

I had felt the impact of this immense vitality the moment I first set foot in Amoy. I came upon it by no rational process, no social studies. I met the tide of lusty and abundant life full in the face, with all its primitive urges undiluted. It was a life, at times, frightening in its force.

It needed to be strong to survive such human miseries as it daily faced.
Mackenzie-Grieves, Gulangyu, 1920s

第四章　厦门精神

厦门人的生活激情　在中国第一年,我们充满了惊奇和激动。我们遭遇了一种内涵丰富无比的陌生文明。一接触这种文明,你马上就会感到震惊、愉悦和困惑,它迅速地改变了我的世界观。这就像第一次打开我所熟悉的光滑表盖,发现里面精致的齿轮在运行,完整、复杂而又持续不断。这是一个完全自给自足的系统,周而复始地转动着,而我自己却从来没有留意。这就要求欧洲人抛弃他们对中国和中国人所抱有的偏见,同时用西方最精华和高级的智慧和文化作为衡量和理解不一样的中国文化及其成就。尽管这个国家的一些现象令人震惊……这些现象背后就是中国,坚固而不朽……

Gulangyu Family, 1920s

一踏上厦门,我就感受到这种巨大生命力的冲击。没有经过理智的思考,也未通过社会学的研究,我承受了这种冲击。我在这里正面遭遇了一种生机勃勃、色彩斑斓的生活,拥有所有纯净的原始冲动。这就是一种生活,能量总是惊人的。

要想在每日所面临的人间苦难中幸存下来,你必须得坚强。

——麦肯兹·格瑞芙于鼓浪屿,20世纪20年代

Old Xiamen
Cradle of Modern Chinese Business & Chinese Business Education

Ancient People of the Future   China is not like ancient Egypt, whose greatness has departed though she still lives on. China is a vital force whose largest possibilities of development lie before and not behind her. A new fresh life is beginning to course through the nation's veins....

Gamewell, 1919

The Magnetic Chinese   The attraction lies in the people themselves, and without any effort on their side the foreigner feels himself drawn by a kind of hypnotism towards them. You cannot explain this and you cannot tell the reason why.

MacGowan, 1907

Gulangyu Friends, 1930s (Bessie Bruce)

一个古老民族的未来　中国不是古埃及。尽管古埃及依然存在,但她伟大的历史已经成为过去。中国是一股充满活力的势力。最大的发展空间还没有成为历史,而是正展示在她面前。一种崭新的生活正在这个国家的血管里流淌……

——甘威尔,1919 年

Amoy, 1892 (John Otte)

磁铁般的中国人　迷人之处在于中国人本身。几乎不费吹灰之力,外国人感觉到自己已经被某种催眠术所控制。你无法解释这种现象,也说不出其中缘由。

——麦嘉湖,1907 年

Old Xiamen
Cradle of Modern Chinese Business & Chinese Business Education

Right Attitude to Life   "Fukien has taught me how to live. Material things can be acquired anywhere in this material world, but an attitude to life can only be mastered in the right environment. Fukien provided such an environment for me."
  Ch'en Sze-ching, Fukien Christian University graduate, 1926 (Scott, 1954)

John Otte and Amoy Christian Endeavor Society, 1891

对待生活的正确态度　福建教会了我如何去生活。在这个现实的世界里,物质的东西随处可取,但对待生活的态度只能在合适的环境中养成。福建给我提供了这样的一个环境。

——陈哲清,福建协和大学1926年毕业生(于苏格兰,1954年)

Old Xiamen
Cradle of Modern Chinese Business & Chinese Business Education

Laughter-Loving Amoy People   The Chinese are a laughter-loving people… There are no people in the world that seem to have such a hypnotizing power over the men of the West as the Chinese. It is not their beauty or their eloquence, nor the fascinating way in which they talk, but in the large amount of human nature they all possess, and in the strain of humour that seems to run through them as music does through an exquisite piece of poetry….

From this it may be easily believed that they are fond of laughter and merriment and the bright and joyous side of things, and social intercourse, and plenty of company, and loud-sounding music and firing of crackers. The solitary feeling that makes an Englishman like to be alone, and shut himself up day after day in a house by himself and not care to see visitors, is something that is quite incomprehensible to a Chinaman….

The Chinese are a humorous and jolly race of people… the position that they hold to-day in the Far East is a signal proof of the vitality and the determined pluck that have carried the Yellow race through the revolutions that during the past centuries have rent and shattered the Chinese Empire.

MacGowan, 1907

Amoy Folk Love Laughter (1907, MacGowan)

商业老厦门
现代中国商业与工商管理教育的摇篮

爱笑的厦门人　　中国人是一个爱笑的民族……世界上没有任何一个地方的人像中国人那样对西方人拥有催眠般的魔力。这不是源于他们的美貌或口才，也不是他们言谈举止极有吸引力，而是很大程度上由于他们所拥有的禀性以及他们浑身上下所散发出来的幽默气质，就像音乐渗入精美诗篇那样自然……

因此，我们有充分的理由相信，中国人喜爱欢笑、快乐以及一切事物的光明和欢乐的一面。他们喜欢社交、爱结伴而行，爱声音大的音乐，爱放鞭炮。对任何中国人来说，英国人所喜欢的特立独行、日复一日地闭门独居、对来客爱理不理，这样的孤独感是很难理解的。

Farmer Tells a Joke, Amoy, 1909 (MacGowan)

……中国人幽默、快乐……他们现在在远东地区所拥有的地位是其活力和坚定决心的一种明显证据。在过去的几百年里，它推动这个黄皮肤的民族通过不断的革命斗争建立或打破了这个中央帝国。

——麦嘉温，1907年

In An Amoy Village, 1933　　J. Nienhuis

Old Xiamen
Cradle of Modern Chinese Business & Chinese Business Education

The Kaleidoscopic Chinese "The Chinese is a person full of surprises. He is like the kaleidoscope, for you feel that whatever strange and unexpected views he may have given of himself you have not yet got the last and final one that will exhaust his character.

MacGowan, 1912

He [the foreigner] was firmly convinced that the white race was superior to the yellow, and they were equally sure of the opposite. When he demanded that they pay respect to science and invention, they countered with an invitation for him to consider the importance of art and literature in the scheme of living.

Lewis, 1938

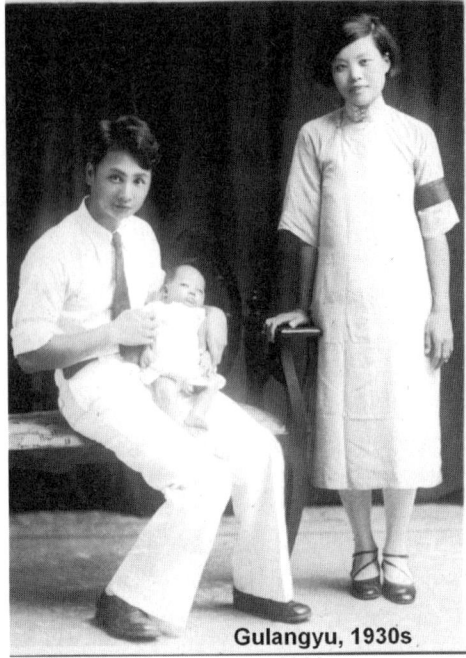
Gulangyu, 1930s

Gulangyu, 1920s

万花筒式的中国人 中国人是一个经常出人意料的民族。就像万花筒,他们向你展示的情景千奇百怪、变幻莫测,但你依然看不到穷尽他们性格的最后招术。

——麦嘉温,1912 年

外国人坚信白种人比黄种人优越,黄种人则恰恰持有相反的观点。当外国人要求黄种人尊重科学和发明的时候,黄种人则请求外国人在生活安排中多考虑文学和艺术的重要性。

——列维斯, 1938 年

Gulangyu Granny, 1907 (MacGowan)

Chinese Band, Amoy, 1908

Amoy Gardener Plays Pipa, 1892 (John Otte)

The Adaptable Chinese

The strength of the Chinaman lies in his power to adapt himself to the circumstances in which he may be situated. Place him in a northern climate where the sun's rays have lost their fire, and where the snow falls thickly and the ice lays its wintry hand upon the forces of nature, and he will thrive as though he had descended from an ancestry that had always lived in a frozen region. Transport him to the torrid zone, where the sun is a great ball of molten flame, where the air is as hot as though it had crossed a volcano, and where the one thought is how to get cool in this intolerable maddening heat, and he will move about with an ease and a comfort just as if a sultry climate was the very thing that his system demanded.

He is so cosmopolitan in his nature that it seems to be a matter of indifference where he may be or what his environment. He will travel along lofty peaks, where the snows of successive winters lie unmelted, or he will sleep in a grass hut where the fever-bearing mosquitoes will feast upon him the livelong night to the sound of their own music, and he will emerge from it next morning with a face that shows that the clouds of anopheles have left him a victor on the field. He will descend into the sultry tin mines of Siam, and at night he will stretch himself on the hard, uneven ground, with a clod for his pillow, and he will rise as refreshed as though he had slept on a bed of down.

MacGowan 1907

Amoy Workmen MacGowan, 1907

适应能力强的中国人 中国人的力量在于他们拥有能够适应各种环境的能力。把他们放在北方,那里太阳不再炎热,积雪深厚,寒冰的魔爪染指大自然,中国人照样人丁兴旺,似乎他们来自远古时代,总是生活在冰封地冻的世界里。把他们放到热带,那里太阳简直就像一团巨大的火球,空气热得跟火山岩浆没有什么两样,常人想的都是如何躲避那令人无法容忍、让人发狂的热气,找到清凉,而中国人却漫不经心、舒适无比地四处走动,好像这酷热的天气正是他们的身体所需要的。

Eight Pounds of Cash Franck, 1925

从本质上来看,中国人四海为家。他们似乎不在意自己身居何处,环境如何。他们会去攀爬冰雪常年覆盖的高峰,或是过夜茅屋,任凭身带热病的群蚊翩然起舞、彻夜叮咬,次日起床一副战场凯旋的模样。白天,他们深入暹罗闷热、潮湿的锡矿。晚上,他们以泥块为枕,凹凸不平的硬地板作床,伸足而眠。第二天起来精神十足,好像前一天是睡在羽绒床上。

——麦嘉温,1907 年

Amoy Boat People, 1921　　　　　J. Nienhuis

Old Xiamen
Cradle of Modern Chinese Business & Chinese Business Education

Evidences of Democracy   The democracy of China is evident from the fact that the people can appeal from the lower to the higher officials, from the higher officials to Peking. The people have exerted their power to put a stop to obnoxious industries; extensive trades have been extinguished, and Imperial examinations discontinued at their demand. Representatives of the people may rise to high offices.

Local reforms are suggested and extensively carried out. There is real popular representation in China on a small scale and locally. The elders in Kwangtung and heads of clans in Fuh-kien, &c., are representatives of the people so far as liability and responsibility to the higher powers are concerned. Even the Emperor is only the "father of his people." He cannot go against the established code nor arbitrarily add to or take from it.

Chinese Recorder, Vol. 20, August, 1889

Chinese Court, 1897 (MacGowan)

民主的证据 中国民主的证据体现在,人民可向各级官员申诉,从基层官员到地方高官,从地方高官到京官。人民行使权力,要求制止某些不良行业发展、大规模贸易行为以及停止殿试。民意代表可以升迁高位。

各种改革在地方发起并广泛开展。真正的民意在中国基层小规模发展。就其对更高一层权力的责任和义务而言,广东省的长老和福建省的族长等等就是这种基层民意的代表。皇上也只是臣民的父王。他不能违背、也不能随意增减既定的礼教习俗。

——《中国教务杂志》,1889年第20卷,第371~373页

A Mandarin, 1892 (John Otte)

Old Xiamen
Cradle of Modern Chinese Business & Chinese Business Education

Ancient Chinese Law "The laws of China," says Dr. Williams, "form an edifice, the foundations of which were laid by Li Kwei twenty centuries ago. Successive dynasties have been building thereon, adding, altering, pulling down, and building up, as circumstances seemed to require. ...The Chinese entertain a profound respect for the laws contained in their national code. "Sir George Staunton remarks that "all the Chinese seem to desire is the just and impartial execution of these laws, independent of caprice and uninfluenced by corruption...."

MacCauley, 1861

October 10th Celebration,   1921, Gulangyu

古代中国的法律　威廉斯博士说:"中国的法律大厦规模宏大,它的基石是由2000多年前的李斯奠定的。历代王朝根据实际情况在他的基础上删删改改,甚至推倒、重盖……中国人对隐藏在礼教习俗里的法律心存敬畏。"乔治·斯汤顿勋爵评论说:"所有中国人希望的似乎是公正无私地执行这些法律,不为变化所动,不受腐败影响……"

——麦考利,1861年

Old Xiamen
Cradle of Modern Chinese Business & Chinese Business Education

Gulangyu

商 业 老 厦 门
现代中国商业与工商管理教育的摇篮

ber 10, 1921　　　　　　　　　　　　　　　　　　J. Nienhuis

Supplement

Eastern Tortoise, Western Hare[①] Amoy, 1900)

By Rev. MacGowan, 1913

(Adapted from *Discover Gulangyu*, by Bill Brown, Xiamen University Press)

The Chinese as a race are on the whole a robust and healthy people. I have no doubt in my own mind that this is largely due to the fact that they have to work for their living…One is surprised in traveling through China at the tireless activity of this people, and I have often wondered how they have been able to endure the wear and tear of successive ages and to be the strong and sturdy people that they are to-day. The simple food they are compelled to live upon, and the health-giving force of daily labor have had the effect of producing a race of people that seem to have all the elements of strength and endurance wrought into the very fiber of their lives.

Amoy

On one occasion a race had been arranged for between two cutters —one managed by an English crew and the other by ordinary Chinese boatmen. The former were men who had been selected with great care from a British man-of-war, whilst the others were men who were daily getting their living by rowing passengers across a broad river. The contest was a peculiar one, for, it was meant to be a test of the powers of endurance of the men of the East and the West, and so it was decided that the course should extend to a large village in the interior nearly twenty miles distant.

Looking at the crews as they sat in their boats waiting for the signal to start, one felt that there could not be the least doubt as to which would be the winner. The bluejackets [British] in their well-known uniform looked the very picture of strength.

Amoy

---

① This boat race (true story!) between the "powerful" British soldiers and their "scrawny" Chinese competitors had an unexpected outcome!

附：
东方龟，西方兔[①]（厦门，1900年）

麦嘉温写于1913年

（摘自《魅力鼓浪屿》，潘维廉著，厦门大学出版社出版）

中国人总体来说是精力充沛和健康的人民。我很肯定，这主要是因为他们为了谋生而工作不息。在中国旅游时，中国人不知疲倦地劳动令人惊叹，我常想他们是如何承受岁月的折磨而变得像现在这样强壮和坚毅的。赖以糊口的粗陋食物，超强的日常劳动强度，造就了这样一个民族，他们的强健和坚韧在生活中随处可见。

(1900, John Otte)

一次，有人安排了一场比赛——参赛的一方是英国水手，另一方是普通的中国船夫。前者是从一艘英国军舰上精心挑选出来的，而后者的工作是每天把行人摆渡到大河对岸。这是一场罕见的竞赛，因为它是东西方男人之间耐力的较量，赛道的终点定在大约20英里外的一个大村庄。

看着水手们坐在船上等待出发信号，毫无疑问英方将取胜。身穿著名蓝色水手服的英国人看起来充满力量。

(1900, John Otte)

[①] 这是一个绝对真实又有趣的故事，讲的是强壮的英国士兵和骨瘦如柴的中国对手之间的一场划船比赛，结果绝对出人意料，敬请欣赏。

They were big, brawny men, with thews and muscles that seemed to be made of iron. These men could never tire, one thought, and there was a proud and confident look on their faces that made one feel that there was no doubt in their hearts as to who should gain the victory.

The Chinamen, on the other hand, with the careless, indolent way in which they are accustomed to hold themselves, gave on the impression that they could never hold out to the end of the journey.

They had never been made to sit upright, and they lounged on their seats as though the whole thing were a vast joke. There was an amused smile on their faces, and they were, no doubt, tickled at the idea that they were going to compete with the famous English, whose deeds of prowess had often been exhibited, to the detriment of their Empire.

At last the signal was given, and away the boats started on their long race. The English got away with a swing, and soon they were far ahead of their Chinese competitors, who continued to row with an even, steady pull upon their oars as though they were quite unconcerned at the rapid progress that the English were making ahead of them.

The beat and the rhythm of the sounds that came from their boat never quickened, nor was there any excitement in the faces of the men, but with a calmness and serenity typical of the East they kept on with their measured strokes, apparently indifferent whether they won or not.

Dragon Boat Race,

商业老厦门
现代中国商业与工商管理教育的摇篮

他们身材高大,肌肉发达,像是钢铁铸成,仿佛永远不会疲倦,脸上流露出的骄傲和自信表明,他们将赢得绝对胜利。

相反,那些中国人一如平时所表现的那样随意懒散,让人感觉他们肯定坚持不到终点。

他们从不坐直身体,而是斜靠在座位上,好像整个比赛不过是一场儿戏。在中国,经常可以见到这些赫赫有名的英国人"累累战功"的破坏痕迹,和他们比赛,着实令中国人感到讽刺,于是大家都面露笑意。

信号终于发出,两条船开始了漫长的赛程。英国人"一桨当先",很快就把中国人远远地甩在后面。中国人则始终平稳匀速地划桨,仿佛一点也不关心英国人正在拉开距离。

他们划船的节奏一点也没有加快,脸上也看不到丝毫兴奋的表情,而是以东方人特有的平和冷静整齐地划桨,显然他们不在乎输赢。

about 1910, MacGowan)

By the time that they had gone ten miles the English crew began to show signs of distress. Their faces were flushed, and their clothes were wet with perspiration, whilst the vigorous swing and dip of their oars with which they had begun the race had lost their naturalness, and were the result of a strained effort that had begun to feel the stress that was laid upon their powers. The Chinese, on the other hand, seemed absolutely unchanged from what they were when they first started. There was no sign of distress on the faces of any one of them, and their pull was steady and regular as though the men were pieces of machinery that were being moved by some invisible force that brought no fatigue upon the rowers.

In the meanwhile the boats were drawing nearer to each other, apparently without any special ef0fort on the part of the Chinese, and finally the latter took the lead and easily came in victors without any signs of strain or fatigue such as were seen in the English crew when the long, exhaustive race was ended.

The Chinese are a strong, sturdy race, with vast physical powers, which have enabled them to successfully endure the wear and tear of constant labor for countless ages. The many days of relaxation that ease the working-men in England are entirely unknown in China. As a Sunday does not exist in that country, they cannot claim the rest of one day in seven which that Christian holiday gives to men in England. There are, indeed, a half dozen or so festivals during the year when people, by universal custom, drop their work and take a holiday, but beyond these labor is continued on every other day in the year…

…But whilst it is perfectly true that the nation on the whole are a healthy, vigorous people, and show no signs of decay in consequence of the incessant toil which every class of worker willingly carries on until old age creeps over him and compels him to take life more easily, it is equally the fact that there is a very considerable amount of sickness to be found existing in any district through which one may be traveling. The casual passer-by would never discover this, for in the bearing of pain and disease the Chinaman is a hero who shows the fiber of which he is made by the quiet endurance with which he suffers and dies if needs be without revealing the agonies that may have made life a torture to him.

船到10英里处,英国水手颓势初现。他们的脸变得通红,衣服被汗水浸湿,出发时有力的摆臂划桨动作也开始变形了,这可不是因为他们感到比赛压力而在故作努力。相反,那些中国人看起来和出发时没什么两样。他们脸上都看不到沮丧,划桨也是坚定有序如同机器一般,仿佛有种无形的力量将他们的疲劳一扫而光。

其间,中国人并没有特别卖力,但两条船越来越近了,最后中国人反超并轻松取胜。经过漫长艰苦的比赛,英国人看上去非常紧张疲劳,而中国人却一点事也没有。

中国人健壮刚毅,体能强大,这让他们能够年复一年地承受持续劳作带来的磨难。英国工人赖以休闲的众多假日在中国是不存在的。这里没有礼拜天,不能像英国人那样,每七天享有一天基督教的休息日。虽然一年中依照民俗,确实有几天节日可以停止工作休息一下,但除此之外的每天,人们劳作不息……

有两种现象在中国是并存的。一方面,全国人民大都健康充满活力,每个阶层的劳动者都任劳任怨,直到上了年纪才不得不干点轻活;另一方面,大量的病患存在于各个地区,但偶然经过的路人永远也不会发现这个事实。因为在忍受病痛方面,中国人堪称英雄。如果需要,他们会默默地承受痛苦和死亡,而不会将烦恼流露,否则生活对他们而言就成了一种折磨。

Fisherman Poles His Boat, 1925 (Franck)

Chapter 5 Amoy's Peace-loving Fighters

Xiamen's Famous Fighters[1]
The Amoy men make good soldiers, so at least it is said; they certainly fought well for their independence, and were the last to yield to the Tartar invaders, and they are those upon whom the conquerors seemed to have pressed most heavily. To this day they wear the turban which they assumed to hide the tonsure and queue imposed on them by the conquerors.

Thomson, 1876

Xiamen Turbans The natives of Fuhkien have always been noted for their independence. They were the last to submit to the foreign yoke of the Manchus,[2] and when the edict went forth for the conquered people to shave the head and wear the pigtail,

Amoy War Junk, 1910 (John Otte)

like their conquerors, they resisted when the rest of China had given in. Thousands lost their heads, rather than wear the queue, and when compelled to yield they wrapped a cloth round their heads to conceal their degradation, and to this day the custom is continued, though its origin is forgotten. This resistance to authority has remained a characteristic of the province.

Johnston, 1898

---

[1] Amoynese were known for being both the most peaceable of Chinese as well as the fiercest of Chinese fighters when their home was threatened—earning them the admiration of even their enemies.

[2] Amoy was the base for Koxinga, the last Chinese hero to rebel against the Manchu invaders; in 1661, he sailed from Amoy and expelled the Dutch from Taiwan, where he died the following year.

商业老厦门
现代中国商业与工商管理教育的摇篮

第五章 热爱和平的厦门斗士

著名的厦门斗士[①] 厦门人可以成为好战士,至少有人这么说过。为了国家独立,他们不懈斗争。他们最迟屈服于满清王朝,也似乎是受征服者的压迫最深重的臣民。直至今日,他们还戴头巾,以掩饰征服者强制他们蓄留的发辫。

——汤姆逊,1876 年

厦门人的头巾 长期以来,福建本地人一直以其独立的个性而闻名。他们是最后屈服于满族统治的汉人。当清朝皇

Amoy People, 1873 Thomson

帝颁发诏书,[②] 要求臣服的汉人像满州人那样剃头蓄辫,中国其他地区的汉人遵从了,而福建人还在反抗。为此,成千上万的福建人宁肯掉头颅,也不愿意留长辫。被强制去发梳辫之后,他们戴起了头巾,隐藏自己的失落。时至今日,这种风俗依然存在,只是缘由已经被人们遗忘了。对执政当局的反抗已经成为这个省份的一个特点。

——约翰斯通,1898 年

[①] 厦门人是中国人中最平和的人,同时当他们的家园遭受威胁的时候,也是最凶猛的斗士。这种矛盾性格甚至连他们的对手也非常敬佩。

[②] 厦门是最后一位抗击满清政府的汉人英雄郑成功的根据地。1661 年,郑成功从厦门启航,把荷兰人赶出了台湾。第二年病逝于台湾。

Might versus Right The soldier occupies the lowest position in the Chinese classification of society, and this arrangement, we think, is in accordance with the true sentiment of the nation on this point. The Chinese do not regard it as at all derogatory to their character to be told that they are deficient in the elements of warlike strength. "We are not a military people," say they, "we are a literary nation. With us reason, and not force, defines rights and privileges; argument, and not the sword, decides controversies."

MacCauley, 1861

Peaceable Amoy Folk The people of this district [Amoy] are exceedingly industrious and peaceable, rowdies excepted, and have never in all the troublesome times, through which this empire has been too often called to pass, disturbed or molested the foreigner or the native Christians. While perchance their love for us is no greater than that of the natives in any other section of this empire, nevertheless they have ever treated us with fairness and commendable hospitality. And in the present calamities [Boxer Rebellion] probably there has not been up to the present time another place in China so undisturbed and so little agitated against foreigners and native Christians as Amoy.

Pitcher, Nov, 1900

Mr. Tan Kah Kee visits Xiamen University in Changting (during Japanese Occupation)
厦大华侨同学欢迎陈嘉庚莅汀视察留影

商业老厦门
现代中国商业与工商管理教育的摇篮

强权与权力　在中国的社会结构中，士兵处于最低层。我们认为，这样的安排与这个国家的真实情感是一致的。如果有人说中国人本质上缺乏好战的实力，他们一点也不会觉得这是对自己人格的一种诋毁。"我们不是尚武的民族，"他们会说，"我们是文明之邦。我们用理智，而不是武力来决定权力和荣誉；我们用争辩，而不是刀剑来解决争议。"

——麦考利，1861 年

热爱和平的厦门人　这个地区（厦门）的人特别勤劳，而且热爱和平。他们不爱热闹。在这个帝国时常经历的困难时刻，他们从不打扰或妨碍外国人或当地的基督教徒。尽管他们对我们的爱护并不比中国其他地方的老百姓更多，但是他们对我们还是相当的公道、友善。在当前的灾难（义和团）中，迄今为止，中国没有一个地方象厦门那样不骚扰外国人和本地基督教徒，不煽动对他们的不满情绪。

——毕腓力，1900 年 10 月

Chinese Sailors in Amoy, 1929

Old Xiamen
Cradle of Modern Chinese Business & Chinese Business Education

Pen Mightier than Sword   Far more formidable than the soldiery are the literati of China. Soldiering is despised in China; learning is esteemed.

Little, 1899

外文系民兵进行高射炮兵训练。这是女高射炮班正在进行对空射击操作。

Girl Students, 1950s, Xiamen University
Foreign Languages Department

Xiamen Univ. Students—forced to wield both pen *and* sword.

商业老厦门
现代中国商业与工商管理教育的摇篮

文字的力量胜过武力
在中国，武士被鄙视，文人受尊敬。因此，比武士更可怕的是文人。
——利特尔，1899年

XMU Student Patrol

"Gun in one hand, books in the other."
Xiamen University Beach, 1950s

XMU Classes in Bombshelter

Old Xiamen
Cradle of Modern Chinese Business & Chinese Business Education

God's Nobility   …there exists in the Chinese soul the material that heroes are made of. The Chinese can suffer and they can die for those whom they love; they can die like martyrs for a cause in which they believe, and to which they have devoted their lives. [1] Arouse the better qualities latent in a Chinese soul, and you will discover one of God's nobility….

Davis, 1896

**Little Gulangyu Refugee, 1938
(Anderson)**

Japanese Ships in Amo

---

[1] When the Japanese occupied Amoy in the late 1930s and 1940s, Xiamen University relocated to the mountains of West Fujian and it was business as usual, even in such austere circumstances. During the 1950s' tense relations with nearby Taiwan, XMU students often held classes in bomb shelters, and were known throughout China for having the slogan, "Pens in one hand, gun in the other." XMU has had more than its fair share of heroic staff and students.

上帝般的崇高　……在中国人的内心深处，有一种造就英雄的东西。中国人能够吃苦，愿意为他们所爱的人去死。他们愿意为自己所信仰的事业献身，直至牺牲自己的生命。① 唤起中国人内心深处潜在的这些优良品质，你会发现他们像上帝般崇高……

——戴维斯，1896 年

Refugee Mother Getting Milk, 1938 (Anderson)

938 (Nurse Jean Nienhuis)

---

① 20 世纪 30 年代至 40 年代，日本人占据厦门的时候，厦门大学迁至闽西山区。尽管条件简陋，学校教学仍正常进行。20 世纪 50 年代，大陆与台湾关系紧张，厦大学生经常在防空洞里上课。他们的口号——"一手拿笔，一手持枪"国人皆知。厦大所拥有的英雄员工和英雄学生的比例超出了正常值。

Old Xiamen
Cradle of Modern Chinese Business & Chinese Business Education

Yellow No Peril[1] Some writers have predicted that a day may come when, inspired by a spirit of war, they [the Chinese] will flash their swords in a wild conquest of the West. This is a dream that will never be realized. Both by instinct and by ages of training, the Chinese are essentially a peace-loving people. The glory of war is something that does not appeal to them. Trade, and commerce, and moneymaking, and peaceful lives are the ideals of the race. No sooner is a clan fight begun, or a war with another nation, than the air at once resounds with the cry, "Mediate," "Mediate." Mediation is in the very blood of the nation, and the man who is a successful mediator is one that wins a golden reputation for himself.

Refugee Child Working

What the West has to fear is not the warlike spirit of the Chinese, which has never been a very important factor in their past history, but their numbers. … The Chinese are a strong race, and can live in comfort, and even luxury, on incomes that would mean starvation to American or Australian workmen.

The battle of the future with the Yellow race will not be fought on any battlefield, but in the labour markets of the nations that they would invade.

MacGowan, 1907

Japanese Gunboat in Amoy, May, 1900 (John Otte)

---

[1] Ironically, even 100 years ago China was dubbed the "Yellow Peril", though it was a dozen Western nations occupying China and not the other way around. MacGowan's observations of the essentially peaceful nature of the Chinese—and the danger of stirring them up—are hopefully as relevant today as when penned over 100 years ago.

黄色非危祸[1]　有些作家预言,将来某一天,中国人在好战精神的鼓动下,会疯狂亮剑征服西方。这是一个永远不会实现的梦想。无论是处于本能,还是岁月的磨炼,中国人本质上是一个爱好和平的民族。战争的荣耀对他们来说没有什么吸引力。贸易、商业和赚钱,以及平静的生活是这个民族的理想。一场家族争斗,或与外国交战刚刚开始,周围的气氛立即回响着"调停"、"调停"的呼声。调停正是这个国家的品性。一个人成功地进行调停就会为自己赢得金子般的声誉。

西方人应该担心的不是中国人的好战精神,而是他们的人口总量,因为战争一直没有成为中国历史上很重要的因素……中华民族是一个坚强的民族。美国或澳大利亚工人认为处于饥饿线的收入,对中国人来说,他们可以过得很舒适,甚至奢侈。

未来与这个黄皮肤民族之间的战争不会发生在任何战场,而是他们可能进入的国家的劳务市场上。

——麦嘉温,1907 年

Refugees on Gulangyu　　　　　J. Anderson

---

[1] 具有讽刺意味的是,100 多年前,中国被蔑称为"黄祸",尽管史实是十几个西方国家占领中国,而非相反。麦嘉温(MacGowan)认为,中国人性格平和,但激怒他们却极为危险。他 100 多年前的评论现在仍然适用。

Old Xiamen
Cradle of Modern Chinese Business & Chinese Business Education

Fujian Governor's 4th of July Toast to U.S.A. & hina

Amoy, 4th of July, 1891

At the celebration of the Fourth of July at Amoy, China, by the Americans, the governor of the province was invited to the banquet, and made a remarkable speech, which shows his intelligence, and suggests some things worthy of consideration.

Tsin Chin-chung was called upon to respond to the toast, "The Emperor of China." In part he said: "China, having followed its own principles of advancement during more than 5,000 years, is now compelled to change and move along European channels. It has begun to own steamships and railways. Its telegraph now covers every province. It has mills, forges and foundries like those of Essen, of Sheffield and of Pittsburgh. China is today learning that lesson in education which Europe has obliged her to learn—the art of killing, the science of armies and navies. Woe, then, to the world if the scholar, profiting by her lesson, should apply it in turn. With its freedom from debt, its inexhaustible resources and its teeming millions, this empire might be the menace, if not the destroyer, of Christendom. No matter what happens, it needs no prophetic gift to know that the 20th century will see at the forefront of the nations of the world—China in the East and America in the West." Well may we pray that, for the welfare of humanity, their purposes will be as peaceful and upright as today.

Chinese Recorder, Vol. 23, January, 1892

Soldiers Drill on Gulangyu After Armistice

福建总督为美国和中国干杯

(1891年7月4日　厦门)

7月4日美国人在厦门庆祝独立日的时候，福建总督应邀出席宴会，并进行了一次出色的演讲。讲话显示了他的才华，并暗示着值得注意的一些事情。

对于为中美友谊干杯，总督作出了回应。他在演讲中说："中国皇帝和中国在遵循自己的原则行事5000多年后，被迫作出改变并按照欧洲人设计的方向前进。我们开始拥有蒸汽船和铁路。电报已经覆盖中国所有的省份。中国的面粉厂、冶炼厂和铸造厂已经跟德国的埃森、英国的谢菲尔德和美国的匹兹堡没有什么两样。今日的中国正在接受欧洲强迫她接受的教育——杀戮的技术：陆、海军的战术。如果学生从所学课程中受益，并反过来用诸实践，那么，对这个世界来说，是一种灾难。以其取之不竭的资源和数万万的人口，一旦还清债务，中国可能成为西方基督国家的威胁，如果不是毁灭的话。无须天才的预言，我们就能看到，无论发生什么，20世纪走在世界最前列的国家——中国在东方，美国在西方。"让我们祈祷，为了人类的幸福、安康，他们的意图是和平的、正直的，就像今天一样。

——《中国教务杂志》，第23卷，1892年1月

Thomson, 1909

Chinese officials at Amoy, Nov., 1908, entertaining officers and crews of American fleet. Admiral Emery proposing health of Empress Dowager

Chapter 6 Gulangyu International Settlement

There are upwards of five hundred European residents at Amoy, for the most part merchants and their families.

Lawrence, 1870

Beautiful Gulangyu   Nothing can be imagined more pleasing, picturesque, and animated than the prospect of the vast mercantile harbor from the heights of Ko-long-soo. The deep channel, crowded with junks, is at the observer's feet; the narrow promontory, forming a chief suburb, projects beyond; further still is the second passage, backed by those noble hills of granite which separate the marine district from the mainland…

Allom, 1843

Beautiful Amoy   September 7, 1841 The next morning (Sept. 7, 1841), Mr. Abeel and myself rose early for a walk around the Island of Kulangsu. It is about three miles long, not quite a mile broad, and is wonderfully diversified with hill and dale. Small as it is, I have never seen so many beautiful prospects in the same space.
   Rev. Walter Lowrie, 1840s

第六章　　鼓浪屿——外国租界

厦门居住着至少 500 个欧洲人，大部分都是商人以及他们的家属。

——劳伦斯，1870 年

美丽的鼓浪屿

从鼓浪屿最顶峰欣赏厦门商港宽阔的景色，你绝对想不出有什么比它更怡人、美妙和生动了。我脚下的这个深水港道泊满了各种船只。小岛的城郊是一片狭长的海角，向远处延伸。再远处就是另外一条航道，背后是宏伟的花岗岩山脉，把海港与大陆分开……

——阿罗姆，1843 年

Nurse Jean Nienhuis

美丽的厦门

1841 年 9 月 7 日

第二天早上（1841 年 9 月 7 日），雅裨理先生和我早早起床，绕鼓浪屿走了一圈。鼓浪屿大致三英里长，不足一英里宽。岛上山峦叠嶂，非常漂亮。尽管面积不大，但我从未在同等大小的地方见过如此众多的美丽景象。

——娄理华，19 世纪 40 年代

Old Xiamen
Cradle of Modern Chinese Business & Chinese Business Education

Scottish Hills of Amoy, May 1860[①]   After dinner, we had a boat-excursion, in company with Mr. J. Stronach, his sister, and young Miss Stronach. This recalled the olden time in Stromness harbor [Scotland]. "We rowed and talked agreeably, though my enthusiasm about the hills…Through many an opening in the rocky hills we saw temples hid among trees, looking so picturesque, built out on jutting rocks. I wish I had my young strength again, to climb at will those mountain rocks and wild romantic paths, all in a state of nature….It is, to my taste, a delightful place, being perfectly surrounded with what I call Scotland's heathery hills. Oh, the flood of beauty tinting those hills when the sun slowly sinks to rest,—when lingeringly it leaves them, and casts its glowing mantle tenderly o'er their rugged rocky sides, softening them to melting beauty.

Jane Edkins, May, 1860

Gulangyu, "Beauty in Miniature"   Across the harbor…is the island of Kulangsu (The Drum Wave Island)… It is exceedingly picturesque…such a diversity of scenery as makes the island one of the pleasantest on the coast of China.

MacGowan, 1897

① The people of Minnan were like the Scottish in many ways, particularly in the way they scattered about the planet and made great contributions in many fields. And interestingly, the Scottish loved Amoy, many of them writing that Amoy's wild terrain reminded them of their rugged Scottish countryside.

苏格兰式的小山，1860年5月[①]　　用过晚餐，我们与约翰·施敦力先生和他的妹妹——年轻的施敦力小姐一起乘船出游。这让我们想起了过去在（苏格兰）斯特罗姆内斯港时的好时光。我们一边划船，一边惬意地聊天，尽管我更关心眼前的这些小山……往石壁林立的小山上看，我们发现许多庙宇。这些庙宇建在凸出的岩石上，隐藏于树林间，看上去美极了。真希望自己依然年轻，精力充沛，可以随心所欲地去攀爬这些山崖，行走在浪漫的野外山路上，所有的这一切都是那么得自然……对我来说，这是一个令人愉快的地方，到处都是我称之为石南丛生的苏格兰小山。噢，当太阳慢慢西斜，美丽的霞光映满群山，或当太阳依依不舍地落到山后，它将夺目的光彩轻轻地洒在峭石林立的山坡上，把山峰软化成令人感动的美丽。

——简·爱德金斯，1860年5月

鼓浪屿＝"微缩美景"　　厦门港正对面……就是鼓浪屿……却是非常得美丽……岛上景观的多样性使得鼓浪屿成为中国沿海最宜人的岛屿之一。

——麦嘉温，1897年

"Camel Rock", Gulangyu, Jan. 1931　　J. Nienhuis

[①] 闽南人在很多方面跟苏格兰人相似。苏格兰人也是在海外寻求财富，并在许多领域做出巨大贡献。特别是在这里——厦门，许多苏格兰人觉得，这里的山水让他们想起了自己的苏格兰故乡。

Gulangyu Ferry, U.S. Consulate in Background (J. Nienhuis)

Getting to Gulangyu   These sampans comfortably seat two, the rower standing in the stern of the boat with his face to the bow, whilst the passengers sit in the front. They are very safe; they cross the harbour in all kinds of weather, and very rarely indeed does an accident happen to them. Of course, when the natives hire a sampan, a great many more than two are crowded into it. Sometimes as many as twelve or fourteen will be seen packed in the bow and in the middle of the boat, until she sinks deep in the water, and it would seem as though with an extra rush of the wave she would sink with her living cargo. Experience has taught, however, that except in severe storms, or whilst the typhoon is raging, when no boat dares to look out even from the narrow creeks in which they have taken refuse, the passage can be made without any risk either to life or to property.

MacGowan, 1897

Boat Carrying Sedan Chair   MacGowan, 1907

上鼓浪屿 这些舢板坐两个人很舒服,划船人站在船尾,面对着船桨,旅客则坐在船头。舢板很安全,可以在任何天气情况下来回穿梭,而且很少会发生事故。当然,本地人租用舢板船的时候,船上就不止两个人了。有时候可以看到12或者14个旅客拥挤在船头和船身直到舢板船吃水很深了,看起来好像再来一个波浪船就会和船上的活货物一起沉入大海。但是,经验告诉他们,这样来回是不会对人或者财产带来任何危险的。除非有非常强烈的风暴,或者是在刮台风的时候,停靠在狭窄湾区避难的船只没人敢开出来。

——麦嘉温,1897年

Amoy Ferry, 1933　　J. Veldman

Old Xiamen
Cradle of Modern Chinese Business & Chinese Business Education

No Vehicles on Gulangyu (1920s) There was no wheeled traffic on Kulangsu: no horses, no bicycles, no rickshaws. Man provided power for sedan chairs, wheel-barrows and carrying poles. The roads, in consequence, were quiet and narrow, running steeply up and down between high-walled gardens.

The noises, except in the streets stretching out from the slipways facing Amoy harbour, were the quick, flat slap of weight-carrying bare feet, the hollow drag and clop of wooden sandals, and always the sound of the sea. The Chinese, with their respect and care for the appropriate name, called it Drum Wave Island. In the small, close-packed town on the harbour, there were Chinese shops, lodgings, little one-storey dwellings, a wall-less theatre, small shrines and temples, linked by waste plots, each ruled by one or more fierce black-tongued chow who waged relentless,

Amoy, Jan. 1934   J. Veldman

blood-spattering battle, until the intruder lay, throat torn out, to rot in the sun, or be gratefully eaten by a poor man's family. Up through an old graveyard and a shimmering acacia grove, one could climb huge granite boulders to the crowning Camel Rock and from it survey the whole island with its square, double-arcaded white houses set in a froth of light and dark green, its too-rare Chinese roofs, its small sandy bays. In summer the green shade was restful; opposite Amoy the mainland coast had long since been stripped of woods.

Mackenzie-Grieve, 1959

Rickshaw at Gulangyu Ferry (Amoy Side), 1934   J. Nienhuis

商业老厦门
现代中国商业与工商管理教育的摇篮

鼓浪屿没有机动车辆（20 世纪 20 年代） 鼓浪屿没有轮式的交通工具：没有马车，没有自行车，没有黄包车。男人抬轿子，推小推车和挑扁担。道路因此安静而狭窄，在高墙深院间高低起伏地延伸。

Edna and Jessie, Hope Hospital Jetty, Oct. 22, 1930　　J. Nienhuis

除了从面对厦门港的船台上沿街传来的声音外，只有负重的赤足急速拍打路面的声音，木屐发出的踢踢答答的声音以及大海的声音。小心择词的中国人将她取名为鼓浪屿。在港口边这个狭小拥挤的小镇上有中国人开的商店、旅馆、单层小房子、露天剧院、小神龛庙宇，中间还夹杂着垃圾堆，每个垃圾堆都由一条或者好几条凶猛的黑舌松狮犬控制。它们没完没了地进行血腥的抢夺战，直到入侵者喉咙被咬断，倒在太阳底下慢慢腐烂，或者被穷困人家心怀感激地当作食物吃掉。穿过一个古老的墓地和一小丛洋槐树，你就可以爬过巨大的大理圆石到最高的骆驼岩（即日光岩，译者注）。在那里可以俯瞰整个小岛，方形而且有双层拱廊的白色房子就伫立在浅色和深绿色的泡沫之上，非常少见的中国式房顶，还有满是沙子的小海湾。夏季绿色的树荫可以让人好好休息，厦门的对面的大陆沿岸则很长时间都没有种植树木了。

——麦肯兹·格瑞芙，1959 年

Hope Hospital "Ambulance", 1920s　　J. Nienhuis

Foreign Consulates [①]
Amoy, the door to the Fookien Province, as its name in Chinese indicates, would be the proper residence for a Consul whose jurisdiction would extend over agents of Swatow [Shantou] and Vice Consuls for the Formosa ports.

Carles, William Le Gendre, U.S. Consul in Amoy, 1871

German Consulate

The elder consuls, we found, invariably liked the Chinese, admired their former achievements, deplored their present situation…and detected the growth of a new national consciousness.

Mrs. Mackenzie-Grieves, British resident of Gulangyu, 1920s

U.S. Consulate, Gulangyu, Summer 1930 J. Nienhuis

---

① Gulangyu had consulates for 14 countries

商业老厦门
现代中国商业与工商管理教育的摇篮

外国领事馆[①]　厦门，就像它的中文意思一样，是福建省的门户，很适合作为领事馆的驻地，管辖区域可以扩展到汕头的代办和台湾港口的副领事。

——李仙得，美国驻厦门领事，1871年

British Consulate　　Pitcher, 1912

我们发现，年长的领事总是喜欢中国人。他们敬仰中国祖先的成就，悲叹当今的状况……并发现了新的国家意识的成长。

——麦肯兹·格瑞芙，20世纪20年代

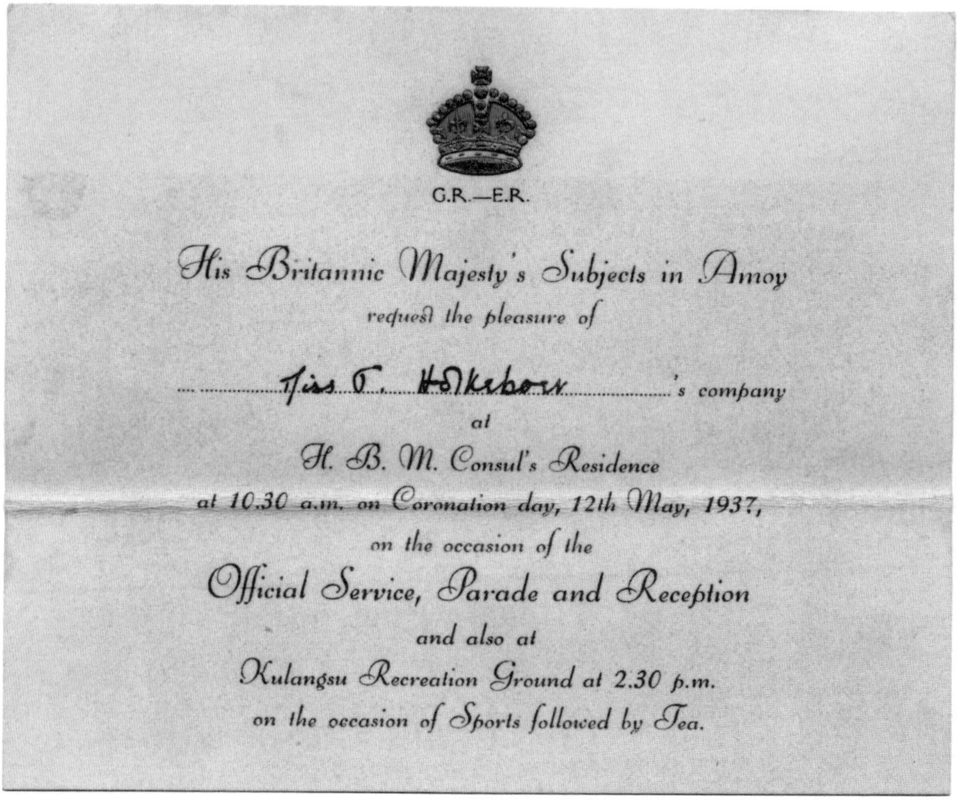

G.R.—E.R.

His Britannic Majesty's Subjects in Amoy
request the pleasure of
Miss T. Holkebozz's company
at
H. B. M. Consul's Residence
at 10.30 a.m. on Coronation day, 12th May, 1937,
on the occasion of the
Official Service, Parade and Reception
and also at
Kulangsu Recreation Ground at 2.30 p.m.
on the occasion of Sports followed by Tea.

---

① 鼓浪屿曾经拥有14个国家的领事馆。

Foreign Law in Xiamen The Island became an international settlement under the control of the Council on May 1, 1903. There is a Mixed Court Magistrate, appointed by the Chinese authorities, who deals with charges brought by the Council or others against Chinese on the island, while foreign offenders are dealt with by their own Consuls.

The Council employs a foreign superintendent of police, who is also secretary to the Council, and a small force of Sikh police. Under this management the island has made progress in many ways, and has become the place of residence, in addition to the foreigners, of a number of wealthy Chinese, who have bought or built foreign houses there.

Like Kulangsu, the British Concession on Amoy has its Municipal Council, consisting of five members elected from the lot holders, who hold their land from the British Government, which rents the whole Concession from the Chinese Government. There is a British inspector of police and a small force of Chinese constables.

Bowra, 1908

A sitting of the mixed court of the International Settlement of Kulangsoo, Amoy.

厦门的外国法律 1903年5月1日，厦门成了在委员会掌控之下的国际租界。这里有中国政府任命的综合治安法庭，处理委员会或者其他人对于岛上中国人提出的诉讼，对于岛上外国人的诉讼则由他们自己成立的委员会处理。

委员会聘用了一位外国警司，同时担任委员会的秘书，还有一小队由印度锡克教徒组成的警察。在这种管理体制下，鼓浪屿在许多方面都取得了进步，不仅仅成了外国人的住地，也成了一些富裕中国人的住地。他们在这里购买或者建造外国式的房子。

Courtesy of Mike Bass and Jill Fowler

就像鼓浪屿一样，厦门岛上的英国租界也有市政委员会，由5位从土地使用者中选取的成员构成。这些成员从英国政府手中租用土地，而英国政府则从中国政府手中租用了整个租界。厦门岛上也有一位警察巡官和一小队中国警察。

——博拉，1908年

The Kulangsu Municipal Police, Amoy.
(C. Berkeley Mitchell, Superintendent, in centre.)

Bowra, 1908

Old Xiamen
Cradle of Modern Chinese Business & Chinese Business Education

International Settlement Committee   A committee is elected every year that has the supervision of the taxes raised from the community, and that has power to repair the old roads and to open new ones. That these committees have acted with great wisdom is evident from the splendid condition of the highways, and also from their extent. Considering the limited area on which they have had to operate, it is very creditable to them that they have managed to make about eight miles of good serviceable roads, which can be used in nearly all weathers.

MacGowan, 1897

Foreign Homes on Gulangyu (1888)   The large luxurious foreign houses are scattered in the most pleasing manner amongst huge madder-colored boulders and rock-masses, shaded by clumps of feathery bamboo, and the flowers or foliage of well-cultivated gardens in a semi-tropical climate. Naturally, in the scorching summer droughts the land does acquire a sickly yellow tone; but in the cooler winter season the island is comparatively green, and here and there a vividly verdant hillside shows where diligent husbandmen have laid out their terraced rice-fields. Carriages and horses are here unknown, their place being filled by chairs and human bearers—strong, patient Chinamen; and boats are ever ready to carry those whose business required their presence to the busy city, which rises so picturesquely on the further shore of the narrow blue strait. To the left lies the harbor; crowded with quaint native junks, wonderful alike in form and color; and a great assemblage of boat-houses, wherein an incredible number of human beings contrive to exist in a much more decent and cleanly way than their neighbor in the streets. On an average, about one thousand foreign vessels annually clear this port.

Dr. John Otte and Family

国际租界委员会 每年都要选举一个委员会负责收取社区的税收，维护旧路，修建新路。委员会的聪明才智很明显可以从公路的良好状况以及长度看得出来。尽管负责的区域有限，他们还是想方设法修建了大约 8 英里公路，路况良好，可在各种气候条件下使用，非常值得称赞。

——麦嘉温，1897 年

鼓浪屿外国人住宅（1888年） 宽敞豪华的外国人住宅精致地散落在茜红色大圆石和岩体之间。一丛丛茂密的竹林，以及亚热带气候条件下精美花园里的花草为他们的住宅遮荫。在炎热、干旱的夏季，大地自然地染上了病态的黄色基调；但是一到凉爽的冬季，鼓浪屿就变得绿意盎然了，到处都是翠绿的山坡，显示了勤劳男人辛勤劳作的成果。这里没有马车，到处都是轿子和强壮、耐心的中国轿夫，随时都有渡船把需要打理生意的人送到喧闹的市区。市区处在狭小的蓝色海峡对岸，从鼓浪屿看过去风景如画。左边是港口，挤满了当地离奇有趣的小帆船，它们的造型和颜色都很接近。还有一大批船屋，上面不可思议地住着一大群人。他们的居住环境比街上的邻居要好得多，干净得多。每年平均有一千艘外国船只到达这个港口。

Dr. John Otte at Home, Gulangyu, 1900

Old Xiamen
Cradle of Modern Chinese Business & Chinese Business Education

As seen from the houses of the foreign residents, the island of Amoy is strikingly picturesque. Though the high, steep hills are in themselves parched and barren ranges of disintegrated granite, they are strewn in every direction with gigantic boulders of the aforesaid rock, which seem as if they could only have dropped from the clouds; though here and there a rocky ridge crops up, cresting the sky-line. One such ridge divides the town itself, and is strongly fortified, heavy guns commanding the estuary where lie so many trading-vessels. Very irregular streets run in and out among the great boulders along the shore, where junks lie stranded, and fine old trees overshadow shrines and temples and nameless graves; the latter being chosen here and there, according to Chinese notions of good luck. ... One point of interest for an afternoon's expedition is a Buddhist monastery, perched on the hillside in this rock wilderness. Stately aloes seem specially to flourish in the soil of decomposing granite, and are thoroughly in keeping with their surroundings.

Miss Gordon Cumming, 1888

Typhoon Villa, Gulangyu, 1892 (John Otte)

商业老厦门
现代中国商业与工商管理教育的摇篮

　　从外国人的住宅看过去,厦门岛风景如画。虽然又高又陡的小山本身就是一堆干透而且光秃秃的大理石块,到处都是巨大而又圆滚滚的大理石岩,似乎就像是天上掉下来的云朵一样。山梁冷不丁地从岩石上冒出来,直插云霄。一道山梁把小镇分成两半。山梁上工事坚固,重武器正对着停靠着很多商船的(厦门)港区。街道蜿蜒穿行在海边的大圆石之间,岸边停靠着小帆船,细细的老树树荫下是庙宇和无名墓地。这些墓地都是根据中国风水来选择的……有个地点适合下午去参观。它是一个佛教寺庙,高高地坐落在这片岩石荒地的山腰上。高大的芦荟似乎特别容易在碎大理石的土地上生长,并完全融入了周围的环境。

——戈登·康明小姐,1888年

Gulangyu, May, 1892 (John Otte)

Gulangyu Family, 1930s J. Nienhuis

Gulangyu's Wealthy Chinese Rich Chinese lived in some, like the family opposite us, but they were mostly those who had had long contact with European merchants or who had made money in the South Seas and, therefore, were not rigidly bound by tradition. Not that they preferred to live among foreigners, but in an International Concession they were better able to safeguard their hard-earned fortunes. Most of them were of humble origin, but the Tan family, whose flowery terrace overlooked our garden, preserved great dignity and a rigid conservatism through their grandfather, who had been a magistrate before the 1911 revolution. In the fine months he was always to be seen sitting among the pots of pink camellias, brush jar and ink slab before him, smoking a long pipe with a minute copper bowl. Occasionally we would meet him, in his long grey silk coat, taking his caged song-bird down to the sea for an airing. He was constantly served by the whole family; filial piety being one of the two basic Confucian principles. But the service was also a genuinely felt tribute to wisdom and experience.

                Mackenzie-Grieve, 1920s

Chinese Gentleman, 1907 (MacGowan)

商业老厦门
现代中国商业与工商管理教育的摇篮

鼓浪屿上富裕的中国人 有些房子是富裕的中国人住的,就像我们家对面的那一家,但是他们大多数都是那些很久以前就已经和欧洲商人有联系,或者已经在南海发了财的人,因此都不是非常严格遵守传统的人。并不是他们喜欢和外国人住在一块,而是在国际租界里,他们可以更好地保护好来之不易的财产。他们大多数人出身卑微。不过,陈姓家族的祖父在辛亥革命之前是一名地方官员,他们保持了守旧的传统。他们家的阳台种满了花草,可以俯瞰我家的花园。天气好的时候,总是可以看到他坐在紫色山茶花盆之间,用带有一个微小铜碗的长烟斗抽烟,面前摆放着毛笔和砚台。

East Meets West in Amoy Clothing
George Koo and his Brothers, 1934

有时候,我们也会碰到他穿着长长的灰色真丝外套,手上提着鸟笼到海边呼吸新鲜空气。他全家人经常要照顾他,孝顺是儒家思想中最基本的两个原则之一。但是,那种照顾也是一种让人真实感觉到的人们对智慧和经验的尊重。

——麦肯兹·格瑞芙,20世纪20年代

Huang Rongyuan Mansion (2008)

Old Xiamen
Cradle of Modern Chinese Business & Chinese Business Education

The Amoy Gazette a daily paper, is printed at one of the two printing-offices in Amoy and laid every evening upon the dinner-table; and during the winter an illustrated comic publication is also issued under the title of *Waffles' Bimonthly*. Ice and aerated waters of various kinds are manufactured upon the island, which now *boasts a "company" formed* with the object of supplying residents with pure unwatered milk.

Add to the above the fact that Koolangsu is in direct telegraphic communication with most parts of the globe, its cheap and varied market, its salubrious climate, and beautiful surrounding scenery; and it will only remain to acknowledge that truly

"The Drum-Wave Island is a paradise on earth;
"The Egret River is second to none!"

Giles, 1878

July 4th Celeb

《**厦门钞报**》 在厦门两家印刷厂之一印制的日报,每天傍晚就可以放到餐桌上。冬天的时候,一份名叫《华夫双月刊》的刊物也会刊登带插图的漫画。岛上生产冰块和品种繁多的汽水,现在发展成了一个"公司",给居民提供未加水的纯牛奶。此外,鼓浪屿和世界大部分地方都保持着电信联络,这里物美价廉、气候宜人、风景优美,我们无法不承认:

"人间天堂鼓浪屿;
鹭江风景甲天下!"

——翟理思,1878 年

on Gulangyu, 1921　　　　J. Nienhuis

Early Xiamen Telecommunications

Close by this sunny spot [Ganzaihou Beach] are the offices of the Great Northern Telegraphic Company, which plays an important part in the life of the Amoy community. Here great questions in commerce are decided in a few seconds, and with the flash of the electric current tidings are sent away to far-distant lands, to bring either pain or gladness to the friends there. Every day the important news of remote countries is talked of and discussed the same day that the events themselves occurred, although they may have happened at the other extremity of the globe. It is a comfort to the foreigner to feel that, though far removed by space from those he loves, he can in any emergency, by stepping down to these offices, come speedily into touch with them, and in the course of a few hours know accurately how they are, and what they are doing.

Macgowan, 1897

NOTICE TO MARINERS.
(No. 10 of the year 1890.)

[The bearings are magnetic, and those concerning the visibility of lights are given from seaward.]

CHINA—EAST COAST.—AMOY INNER HARBOUR.

Time Signal at North Point of Kulangseu.

INFORMATION has been received that a time signal has been established on the north-eastern slope of Wellington's Nose, northern point of Kulangseu, Amoy Inner Harbour:—

The signal is a gun, which is fired on Wednesdays and Saturdays, at noon, Amoy Custom House mean time, equivalent to 16h. 7m. 43·9s. Greenwich mean time.

The flag T of the International Code is hoisted at the flagstaff about 5 minutes before signal, and hauled down at the instant of the signal. Should there be any error in the signal, the flag is kept at half-mast for 10 minutes.

Position of signal, latitude 24° 27′ 25″ N., longitude 118° 3′ 33″ E.

By command of their Lordships,
W. J. L. Wharton, Hydrographer.
Hydrographic Office, Admiralty, London,
3rd January, 1890.

Gulangyu Cannon, 1920s — J. Nienhuis

商业老厦门
现代中国商业与工商管理教育的摇篮

早期的厦门电信服务　　就在这个阳光明媚的地方（港仔后海滩）附近就是大北方电信公司的办公室。这里对于厦门人的生活起到了举足轻重的作用。很多重要的商业问题在这里几秒钟内就决定了，并通过闪电般快捷的电流发送到遥远的地方，给那里的朋友带去痛苦或者开心的消息。就在事情发生的当天，遥远国度的重要新闻每天都被谈起或者讨论，就像在国内一样，即使事情是发生在地球的另一端。对于外国人来说，这是一种安慰，尽管他们在空间上远离亲人，但是在紧急情况下，他们就可以走进这里，迅速地和亲人们取得联系，几个小时之后就可以准确了解亲人们的情况，目前从事的工作等等信息。

——麦嘉温，1897年

AMOY--SKETCHED FROM THE SIGNAL STATION

Amoy Union Club on Gulangyu The spacious edifice now occupied by the members of "The Club" was erected in the year 1876, to replace some very inconvenient premises that had done duty for a number of years previously, before the community had increased to its present numerical proportions. The building contains a fair library, a reading-room supplied with all the best home and local papers, a billiard-room with two tables, a bowling-alley, a bar for drinks and oysters, and a committee-room, which last is nightly used for the table d'hote at 7:30 P.M. The latest telegraphic news of steamers dispatched to and from the various coast ports is published in the hall, where an excellent barometer is kept for the information of those interested in the changes of the weather…

Attached to the Club is a small theatre, in which a number of excellent performances are given during the winter season, many of the ladies kindly lending their assistance. The racquet-court stands alongside of the theatre, and is an inexhaustible source of health to all who can stand this severe exercise. At no great distance is the Recreation Ground, whereon some goodly cricket may be seen during the cool months. There is one annual Race Meeting, which lasts two days, and is held upon the Amoy side of the water. Extremely good shooting is to be got in the neighbourhood, where geese, duck, teal, and snipe, may be bagged in large quantities. Lawn Tennis is played both in public on the Recreation Ground and in private at the residences of those who are fortunate enough to possess available lawns. The harbor is admirably adapted for boat-sailing, and the walks round Koolangsu are pretty if somewhat monotonous.

The fine sandy beaches are devoted during the hot months to evening walks and talks, followed by a plunge in the sea as the shades of evening begin to draw…

Giles, 1878

The Recreation Ground and Masonic Hall, Kulangsoo, Amoy.

Postcard Courtesy of Mr. Ashley Brewin

鼓浪屿上的俱乐部　俱乐部成员现在使用的那座宽敞大厦建于1876年,用来取代已经使用多年、且极其不方便的旧楼。之前,社区人口也没有目前这么多。大楼里有一个不错的图书馆,一间拥有国内和当地最棒的报刊阅览室,有一间台球室,里面放着两张台球桌,一条保龄球道,一个供应饮料和生蚝的吧台和委员会的办公室。委员会办公室每晚七点三十分成了吃饭场所。来往于各个港口轮船的最新电报消息公布在大厅里。那儿还放了一支极好的晴雨表,为那些关注天气变化的人服务……

小剧院是俱乐部的附属建筑之一。冬季,那里有很多精彩的表演,许多友好热情的女士给了慷慨的资助。网球场就在剧院的旁边。对于那些能够承受如此剧烈运动的人来说,它无疑是一个取之不尽、用之不竭的健康资源。健身场距俱乐部不远。在凉爽的季节里,人们能在那儿看到精彩的板球比赛。

每年,厦门海岸边都会举行一场为期两天的赛马大会。附近还有一个非常棒的猎场,可以捕获大量的鹅、鸭、水鸭,还有沙锥鸟。有人在公共健身场上打草地网球,也可以在自家的草地上打。港口非常适合划船,绕着鼓浪屿步行,虽说有点单调,但还是很舒服的。

夏季傍晚时分,人们在美丽的沙滩上散步和闲谈。夜幕降临时,人们跳入海中……

——翟理思,1878 年

Old Xiamen
Cradle of Modern Chinese Business & Chinese Business Education

Foreigners Loved Life in Old Amoy

"Oh! if I were but back in Amoy!"

Dr. Young in his last days
(Barbour, 1855)

Swimming in Amoy, 1920s J.N.

The "Jolly Six", 1924 J. Nienhuis

Gulangyu Tennis, 1920s J. Nienhuis

老外热爱老厦门的生活

"噢！要是我能再回到厦门！"
——杨格博士
（临终前在巴伯尔说，1855年）

Young John Finds Baby Amoy Tiger in Backyard (Amoy, 1920s, Bessie Bruce)

"Amoy Bus Tour," Zhongshan Park, Dec. 10th 1930   J. Neinhuis

Some of the 100s of foreigners who called Amoy home....

DePree Family, Spring, 1932 (in Amoy 1907 to 1948) J.N.
Henry, David "Pitts," Kate, "Harold "Pewee", and Catherine B.

J. Nienhuis
Peder and John Vandeweg
Family in Amoy from 1919-1926
(Their father, a surgeon, died in Amoy)

Horace Day (later famous American artist) and Siblings

**Dr. Hofstra and Family
In Amoy 1922-1951**

The Koeppe Family (in Amoy from 1919-1951)

在这几百名外国人中，有些人称厦门为自己的故乡……

Stricks (Amoy 1911-24) and Hofstras (Amoy 1922-51)

Nurse J. Nienhuis (center) In Amoy 1922-1951

Veenschoten Family (1928), in Amoy 1917-1951
(Daughter Joann and Husband returned, 1947-1951)

Dr. Bosch and Family, 1920s   J. Neinhuis

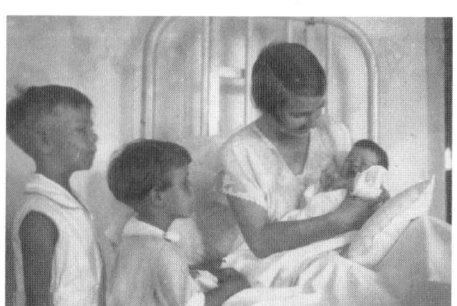
Mrs. Taylor and Children, 1920s (J. Nienhuis)

Prince Henry Visits Amoy
1900 (John Otte)

商业老厦门
现代中国商业与工商管理教育的摇篮

New Year, Gulangyu, 1936
Photo Courtesy of J. Anderson

New Years Celebration, Gulangyu, 1938
Photo Courtesy of John Anderson (whose parents are the Gypsy and Snowman)

Sports in Old Amoy

老厦门的体育

Amoy Horse Races *Outing, Volume 16, 1890*

Jeans, 1897
Golf in Gulangyu Graveyard, 1880s

BOAT RACES IN THE INNER HARBOUR OF AMOY.

AQUATIC SPORTS AT AMOY
"The Graphic," Nov. 3, 1883

Old Xiamen
Cradle of Modern Chinese Business & Chinese Business Education

Camel Rock[①] (1940s)   Walking up a sun-steeped lane, I came to the highest point and centre of the island, known as Camel Rock....

Around this sleeping motionless camel were clustered tier upon tier, rows of red and drab-white brick houses, criss-crossed by a series of narrow lanes which could not be travelled either by car, bicycle, or rickshaw. The only equipage available on Kulangsu were some old sedan chairs, but even these were sparingly used and principally by pregnant women on their way to the mission hospital when they felt their critical hour was approaching. Scattered shops lay at one end of the island in which

U.S. Sailors on Gulangyu

fat shopkeepers were dozing away their siesta houses in long easy chairs, lazily fanning themselves in a state of coma...About fifty foreigners of many nationalities still lived here together with retired Chinese officials, professional men and the wealthier merchants whose interests lay on the Amoy side but who preferred the greater quiet of Kulangsu...

Foreigners were advised not to stay on Amoy Island after dusk. Nothing had ever happened, but one day it might.

Neill, 1956

Drum Rock, Gulangyu, 1920s (Dorothy and John Day)

---

① Today, called Sunlight Rock, 日光岩

骆驼岩[①]（即现在的日光岩）
（20世纪40年代） 走过洒满阳光的巷子，我来到了岛上最高点和中心点，也就是著名的骆驼岩……

聚集在这头丝纹不动的睡骆驼周围的是一间间红色和褐白色相间的砖房。一条条狭窄的巷子相互交错，汽车、自行车和人力

Tour Group, 1920s   J. Nienhuis

车都无法通行。鼓浪屿上唯一可用的设备是种古老的轿子，但是也很少人使用，主要用于怀孕的妇女感觉快要生的时候才坐上轿子赶往传教士医院。岛屿的另一头有一些商店。胖乎乎的店主躺在长椅上睡午觉，昏睡时还慢慢地摇着手上的扇子……大约有50位来自世界各国的外国人和退休的中国官员住在这里，也有一些专业人士和富裕商人喜欢鼓浪屿的安静。所以，他们也选择住在鼓浪屿，虽然他们需要打理的事情都在厦门岛上…

有人建议外国人在黄昏之后都不要在厦门岛逗留。虽什么事都还没有发生，但是也许某一天就会。

——尼尔，1956年

Conquering Camel Rock, Gulangyu, 1920s   J. Nienhuis

---
① 如今，它被称为日光岩。

THE YOUNG PRINCES ON THEIR CRUISE—A PICNIC AT "THE TEMPLE OF TEN THOUSAND ROCKS," ON AMOY ISLAND

THE GRAPHIC, FEB. 11, 1882

商 业 老 厦 门
现代中国商业与工商管理教育的摇篮

Touring Amoy Countryside, 1924   J. Nienhuis

Amoy Bus, 1924   J. Nienhuis

Chapter 7 Xiamen—Cradle of Modern "Chinese"① Education

Xiamen's Pioneer Educators
There was no lack of congenial companionship, for this [Amoy] was the rallying point of that picket line of educational pioneers in Asia, who began the work whose fruits are seen today. In later years, in Japan, Dr. Hepburn delighted to tell about his early life at Amoy, where he was intimate with Morrison, Milne, Medhurst, Muirhead, Peter Parker, Abeel, Walter Lowrie, Bridgman and Culbertson.

Griffis, 1913

Given Amoy's excellent harbor, its entrepreneurial populace, its intimate connection with the far-flung Amoy Network, and its use of the Chinese dialect already spoken by most foreigners abroad, it was no surprise that merchants, missionaries and diplomats② came first to Amoy, and within a mere six decades Gulangyu was touted as the "richest square mile on earth." But in Amoy, as elsewhere in China, political upheaval and war with the Japanese took its toll. By the 1940s, Amoy's elite had fled abroad, taking their wealth with them, and Gulangyu's hundreds of elegant mansions began their decades-long descent into decay

---

① There were of course early modern schools in Shanghai and Bejing, but Xiamen was unique for its very early cooperation between Chinese and foreigners in implementing programs suited to China (and, of course, Xiamen University was the first such university started by an Overseas Chinese, for the Chinese, and it pioneered Chinese business education).

② Even as late as the 1949, Western powers sent junior officials to Amoy for language study to prepare them for diplomatic service in other Asian countries such as Malaysia or Singapore.

第七章　现代中国教育的摇篮[①]

厦门——亚洲现代教育的先驱　现代教育中不缺志同道合的同伴。厦门跑在亚洲教育先驱战线上的首位,如今已见成果。后来在日本,赫伯恩博士很高兴地谈起其早年在厦门的生活。在那里,他和莫里森、米尔恩、梅德赫斯特、缪尔黑德、彼得·帕克、阿比尔、沃尔特·洛雷、布里奇曼和库伯森成为莫逆之交。

——格里费斯,1913 年

厦门拥有优良的港口和富有冒险精神的人民。她与广布海外的厦门商人圈关系密切,所使用的方言已经广为外国人所接纳。难怪外国商人、传教士和外交官会首先登陆厦门。[②]在短短的六十年里,厦门就被誉为"地球上最富庶的平方英里"。

然而,厦门跟中国其他地方一样,在政治纷争和日本侵略中遭受损失。到了20世纪40年代,厦门的精英纷纷带上财富,逃亡海外。鼓浪屿岛上数以百计的雅致公馆开始了长达数十年的没落、衰败。

Young Scholar in Official Dress (MacGowan, 1907)

---

① 上海和北京当然也有中国早期的现代学校。但是,厦门与众不同之处在于她很早就开始与外国人合作开设适合中国的课程(当然,厦门大学就是这样一所有华侨创办、为中国人服务的大学。她是中国工商教育的开路先锋)。

② 近至1949年,西方国家还派出过低级官员到厦门学习闽南话,以便他们将来可以到诸如马来西亚或新加坡等其他亚洲国家从事外交工作。

Old Xiamen
Cradle of Modern Chinese Business & Chinese Business Education

Amoy's True Wealth From all outward appearances, Amoy had lost its place in the sun. But the island city's true wealth had never been its money but the spirit of the people who could overcome adversity to thrive and prosper, whether at home or abroad. And these "Yankees of China's" greatest and most lasting influence was not in commerce but in helping to pioneer China's modern education—an investment in the future that is paying great dividends for the entire nation even today.

Girl Students,

厦门真正的财富　从所有的表象上来看,厦门已经失去了她在世界上的地位。然而,这个岛城的真正财富从来就不是金钱,而是岛民的精神。无论在国内,还是在海外,他们都能克服逆境,兴旺发达。这些"中国的扬基人"最伟大而深远的影响不在于商业,而是开创了中国的现代教育。时至今日,这种面向未来的投资对整个国家的回报是巨大的。

u, 1921 (Jean Nienhuis)

Old Xiamen
Cradle of Modern Chinese Business & Chinese Business Education

Chinese—Lovers of Learning
Amoy's missionaries found a ready audience for their education reforms. Foreigners had long called China the "Land of Books" because Chinese valued education and learning perhaps higher than any other peoples—and nowhere was this truer than in Fujian province.

Fujianese Dominate Academics
Although Chu Hsi, one of China's greatest philosophers, was a Fukienese, and, as a Foochow scholar pointed out to me, in the Chinese equivalent of the *Dictionary of National Biography*, one hundred and sixty-one out of the two hundred and eighty-two biographies

Scholars are much revered in China

are of Fukienese...
  Mrs. Avril Mackenzie-Grieves,
  British resident of Gulangyu, 1920s

Land of Books China is said to have more books than any other country. I am not able to say whether this statement is true or not, but certainly the Chinese have a voluminous literature. In Peking there are several blocks of streets in the Chinese city which are devoted to books. The Hanlin Library [1] contained many thousand volumes. Among them there was one work comprising 23,633 volumes...
  Denby, 1906

One Chinese Page = One Western Volume
"...the Chinese classic masters express their wisdom with such succinct clarity that a page from their works is as full of meat as a volume of Western philosophy."
  Mrs. Averil Mackenzie-Grieves

Young Amoy Scholar, 1930s

---
[1] China's first public library was in our Fujian Provincial capital of Fuzhou

商业老厦门
现代中国商业与工商管理教育的摇篮

中国人——知识的爱好者　传教士为他们的教育改革找到了现成的对象。外国人很早以前就称中国为"书籍之乡",因为长期以来中国人比其他任何民族更加重视教育和知识。这在福建尤为真实。

福建人的学术成就独占鳌头　朱熹,中国最伟大的理学家之一,是福建人。一位福州学者告诉我,《中国名人大词典》(相当于《英国名人词典》)里,282个名人传记有161位福建人……

——麦肯兹·格丽芙,英国女士,20世纪20年代居住鼓浪屿

书籍之国　中国据说拥有比其他国家更多的书籍。这种说法是否真实,我无从考究。不过,说中国文学书籍浩瀚如烟海却是无庸置疑的。在北京,好几个街区的生意与书籍有关。① 翰林院藏书数以千计。其中,有一部著作多达13633卷……

——田贝, 1906年

中国一页＝西方一卷　……中国古代大师善用简洁的语言表达思想。他们一页作品的信息量相当于一卷西方哲学书。

——麦肯兹·格丽芙,英国女士,20世纪20年代居住鼓浪屿

Second Hand Bookvendor, 1934

---
① 中国的第一座公共图书馆就坐落在福建省会城市福州。

Old Xiamen
Cradle of Modern Chinese Business & Chinese Business Education

Faith in Education The Chinese have a profound faith in education. High and low and rich and poor are absolutely of one mind on this point, and if a boy is not sent to school, it is either because the parents are too poor, or because they have not sufficient authority over him to compel him to study. One need not be surprised at this unanimity of opinion, for education is the royal road to the honours and emoluments that the State has to bestow, and it is by means of it that the wildest ambition that ever ran riot through a young man's brain can ultimately be satisfied. In the West there are many ways by which a man may rise to eminence…In China they are all narrowed down to one, and it is the one that leads from the schoolhouse.

MacGowan, 1913

Like a Beehive--Endless Rows of Imperial Exam Cells (Fuzhou, 1890s, John Otte)

Entrance to Imperial Examination Halls (Fuzhou, 1890s, John Otte)

商业老厦门
现代中国商业与工商管理教育的摇篮

重视教育 中国人对教育极为重视。在教育的问题上,无论贫富、尊卑,他们的想法是完全一致的。小孩不上学,要么是父母亲太穷,要么是他们没有足够的威信来强制孩子读书。对教育问题的一致看法,你不用感到奇怪,因为它是通往国家所赋予的荣耀和奖赏的最佳线路。通过这个办法,野心勃勃的年轻人最终能够实现自己的理想。在西方,通往成功的路径千千万……在中国,只有教育这座独木桥,它的起点就在学堂。

——麦嘉温,1913年

Old Xiamen
Cradle of Modern Chinese Business & Chinese Business Education

The Amoy Mission and Education

Christians in Xiamen (1700)   There are about fifty Christians in Amoy, and they have a chapel served by French missionaries...
      Hamilton, 1727

Xiamen—the Mother Church   In 1872 we find that the Mission to Amoy has expanded into three distinct centers [Xiamen, Shantou, Taiwan], independent of each other, but under the one home Committee of management. Amoy may justly claim to be the mother of them all; it was from that, as the original headquarters, that they took their departure.
      Johnston, 1898

Rev. David Abeel
1st Amoy Missionary

Amoy's "Bamboo Church", 1921

厦门传教和教育

基督教在厦门（1700 年）　厦门大约有 50 个基督教徒，他们有个教堂，教堂由法国传教士提供服务。

——哈密尔顿，1727 年

厦门——母教堂　1872 年，厦门传教团发展扩大成三个相互独立的中心（厦门、汕头和台湾），但同归一个教会组织管理。厦门可称为它们的母亲，从那以后，它们各自作为当地的总部独立发展。

——约翰斯通，1898 年

Kho Seng-lân bok-su and 2 Preachers

Meeting of 3 Missions (English Presbyterian, London Mission, Dutch Reformed) Amoy, 1892

Old Xiamen
Cradle of Modern Chinese Business & Chinese Business Education

Amoy's Pioneering Education began with the arrival of China's first Protestant missionaries in 1841. Although their primary goal was missions, they did much more than just build China's first Protestant churches, or its first medical mission.① Many foreign missionaries lived in Amoy for several decades, and avidly filled their leisure hours studying Fujian history, culture, language, botany, biology, geology. As years and decades passed, what began as mere hobbies quite often ended with groundbreaking contributions to everything from Fujian ornithology to Minnan map-making.②

Girls' School, December, 1891 (John Otte)

Roots of Pinyin in Amoy (July 14, 1851) "The plan is yet only an experiment, but seems perfectly feasible. We trust that, by some such means as this, much may be done towards the elevation of the great mass of this people. By the use of their present cumbersome characters, the great majority can never become intelligent readers; but by the plan thus adopted, if we can only furnish the requisite number of books, the means of learning to read will be within the reach of almost every individual.

Talmage Letter to Anderson and De Witt

---

① Gulangyu is also the "Cradle of Tropical Medicine; it was here that Patrick Manson was the first to connect mosquitoes with elephantiasis (1878) and malaria (1894), and discovered that only female mosquitoes suck blood (males live on fruit juices). A doctor in England said Manson's claims were "either the work of a genius or, more likely, the emanations of a drunken Scots doctor in far-off China, where, as everyone was aware, they drank too much whisky."

② Even today, many leading Western museums have displays of these missionaries' discoveries in Amoy-related subjects.

商业老厦门

现代中国商业与工商管理教育的摇篮

厦门教育的先驱 厦门的教育始于1841年第一批新教传教士抵达中国。① 尽管他们的主要目的是传教,但他们所做的远不止建设中国第一座新教教堂,或第一家教会医院。许多外国传教士在厦门生活数十年。他们如饥似渴地研究福建的历史、文化、语言、植物、生物和地理,以充实自己的闲暇时光。多年过去了,起初只是个人嗜好的研究常常变成了对福建从鸟类学到闽南地图绘制等方方面面具有划时代意义的贡献。②

65 of Miss Johnston's Students Who Became Teachers (1907, Johnston)

拼音的根在厦门(1851年7月14日) 这个计划还只是一个实验,但看起来完全可行。我们相信,通过类似的办法,提高这个民族广大人民群众的素质,可做的事情很多。他们现在使用繁琐的字符,永远不可能变成有思想的读者。采用这个计划,只要我们提供足够数量的书籍,每个人都可以学会阅读。

——塔尔米奇致安德森和德·韦特的信件

---

① 鼓浪屿也被称为"热带医学的摇篮"。在这里,曼森是第一个把蚊子和象皮病(1878年)及疟疾(1894年)联系在一起的人。他还发现,只有母蚊子才吸血(公蚊子靠吸取植物的汁液维持生命)。一名医生在英国说:"曼森的论断像是一位天才的工作成果,但更像是一个远在中国的醉酒的苏格兰医生所说的胡话。众所周知,他们在中国喝威士忌有多么凶。"

② 许多西方著名的博物馆至今仍在展示这些传教士在厦门发现的相关内容。

Old Xiamen
Cradle of Modern Chinese Business & Chinese Business Education

Amoy Dialect in Braille   In the adaptation of Braille, which has been made to the Amoy Vernacular, the letters of the alphabet are full-length, thus leaving the tonal marks to be formed from upper and middle dots and the punctuation from middle and lower ones. The letters are combined phonetically —and also as initials and finals—to spell out the short monosyllabic words, which, on an average, require only three letters and a fraction to each. Of course the Braille figure-dots are kept for the use they were originally intended to serve.

Amoy Dialect in Braille
EDUCATION AND WORK FOR THE CHINESE BLIND.
[Chinese Recorder, Vol. 21, 1890]

ç k p t a e i o u n

ch kh ph th aⁿ eⁿ iⁿ oⁿ uⁿ ng

... It may be well to state that, for beginners, it is advisable to have guides made that will produce dots standing slightly more apart than those from the ordinary standard pattern. Failing this, a very good way of giving lessons on the formation of letters and words is to work with short wooden pins on the octagonal board which the blind use for arithmetical exercises.* The pins ought to have the ends smoothly rounded, and be cut to fit the holes exactly, the readiest way of making them being from bamboo splints. Pupils whose hands have become hardened by manual labour, should leisurely wash them with soap and warm water before commencing to read.

Campbell, 1889

Xiamen's Pioneering Women's Education   In 1845, Rev. Lyman Burt Peet (弼来满) started China's first day-school on Gulangyu, and William Young (养为霖) opened Fujian's 1st school for girls about the same time. One of China's first kindergartens, Gulangyu Huaide Kindergarten (鼓浪屿怀德幼儿园), was built in early 1898.

Gulangyu Students, 1933

商业老厦门
现代中国商业与工商管理教育的摇篮

Girls going to school, Gulangyu

盲文的厦门方言 盲文的改写本已按厦门本地方言编制，字母是标准长度，因此声调由上方和中间的圆点构成，标点符号从中间和下方的圆点形成。文字按发音组合，同时按首字母和最后的字母组合，这样就可以拼出单音节的短词。这些短词平均只需要用三个字母和一个符号。当然，盲文中的数字点依然保留其原有的功能。

——坎佩尔，1889 年

厦门女子教育的先驱 1845 年，弼来满牧师在鼓浪屿创办了中国的第一所日间上课的学校。大致同一时间，养为霖开办了福建的第一所女子学校。鼓浪屿怀德幼儿园创办于 1898 年，是中国最早成立的幼儿园之一。

Gulangyu Girl's School

Amoy Girls' School, May, 1892 (John Otte)

"Ten years ago," writes Miss M.E. Talmage, of Amoy, "there were comparatively few Christian women in this region who could read the Scriptures, and the pupils in girls' schools were but a few score. This year (1902) there are seven hundred girls under instruction, while there are over a thousand women who can read."

The Outlook, August 1, 1903

商业老厦门
现代中国商业与工商管理教育的摇篮

Gulangyu Girls' School, Oct. 1933

打马字·马利亚小姐曾这样描述厦门："十年前，在这个地区，只有少数几个基督教妇女能读基督教经文，女子学校有女生，但只有一二十个。今年（1902年）有700个女生接受教育，一千多妇女能阅读。"

——《瞭望》，1903年8月1日

All-Xiamen Girls' Volleyball Champions, 1932   J. Nienhuis

China's First Mission Medical Work and Medical Education

Amoy—1st Medical Missions in China   The year 1844 is a noted one in the history of medical missions.   In January Drs. Hepburn and Cummings opened a hospital in the city of Amoy…

Chinese Recorder, Volume 5, Shanghai, Volume 5

Gulangyu's Pivotal Role in Modern Medicine

Adapted from *Discover Gulangyu*　（《魅力鼓浪屿》）

For such a minor islet, Gulangyu has played a major role in developing modern medicine. On Gulangyu, "The Cradle of Tropical Medicine（热带医学的摇篮）," Sir Patrick Manson（帕特里克·曼森先生）made his great medical discoveries, and little Gulangyu gave birth to Lin Qiaozhi（林巧稚）, "Mother of China's dern Obstetrics and Gynecology."

Gulangyu's trailblazing medicine began in 1842 with the arrival of Dr. Cummings, who lived with Amoy's first missionary, David Abeel (Yabili, 雅裨理), in the old home at #23 Zhonghua Rd. The two later moved to Liaozihou（寮仔后）and then to Zhushujiao（竹树脚）, where in 1843 they founded a clinic that was forerunner of "Chibao（赤保）hospital" (later part of Hope Hospital).

Gulangyu's honor roll of medical missionaries includes pioneers like Dr. J.C. Hepburn (1843-1845), Dr. James Young (English Presbyterian Mission, 1850-1854), Dr. Hirschberg (London Missionary Society, 1853-1858), and Dr. John Carnegie (1859-1862). But my favorite of the lot is Dutch-born American Dr. John Abraham Otte (Yu Yuehan, 郁约翰), of the American Reformed Mission [①] (Guizheng Jiao, 归正教).

Dr. Otte Operating with Chinese Assistants

---

① ARM, known as the Reformed Protestant Dutch Church from 1816-1826.

商业老厦门
现代中国商业与工商管理教育的摇篮

中国第一家教会医院和医学教育机构

厦门——中国最早开办教会医院的地方　1844年是教会医院历史上值得注意的一年。当年一月，赫伯恩和康明两位医生在厦门设立了第一所医院……

——《中国教务杂志》，第五卷，上海

鼓浪屿在中国现代医学的重要地位（摘自《魅力鼓浪屿》）

鼓浪屿这个弹丸小岛在现代医学的发展过程中扮演了重要的角色。正是在这"热带医学的摇篮"，帕特里克·曼森先生取得了重大的医学发现；小小的鼓浪屿还诞生了"中国现代妇产科之母"林巧稚。

鼓浪屿对医学的贡献始于1842年。那年，鼓浪屿来了两个人——康明医生和第一个进入厦门的传教士雅俾理。他俩合住于现在的中华路23号一座舒适的旧屋。这对搭档后来搬到寮仔后，之后又搬到竹树脚。在那儿，于1843

Photo Courtesy of Wellcome Library, London
Sir Patrick Manson, "Father of Tropical Medicine," Amoy, 1881

年开设了一家诊所，就是"赤保医院"的前身（后来成为"救世医院"的附属医院）。

早期在鼓浪屿悬壶济世的传教士包括J.C.赫伯恩(1843-1845)医生，英国长老会詹姆士·杨格医生(1850-1854)，伦敦差会赫希堡医生(1853-1858)，和约翰·卡内基医生（1859-1862）等先驱者。不过，所有人中，我个人最为推崇的是生于荷兰的美国人，归正教（ARM）[①]的郁约翰博士。

---

① ARM，在1816-1826年间被称为归正教。

181

Hope and Wilhelmina Hospital (Men's on Rt. Women's on Left)
Hospital Chapel 1 story bldg. in Center; nurses home on hill in back

Hope and Wilhelmina Hospitals' Staff, 1932 (Jean Nienhuis)

商业老厦门
现代中国商业与工商管理教育的摇篮

Dr. Otte With Students, Graduates and Their Families

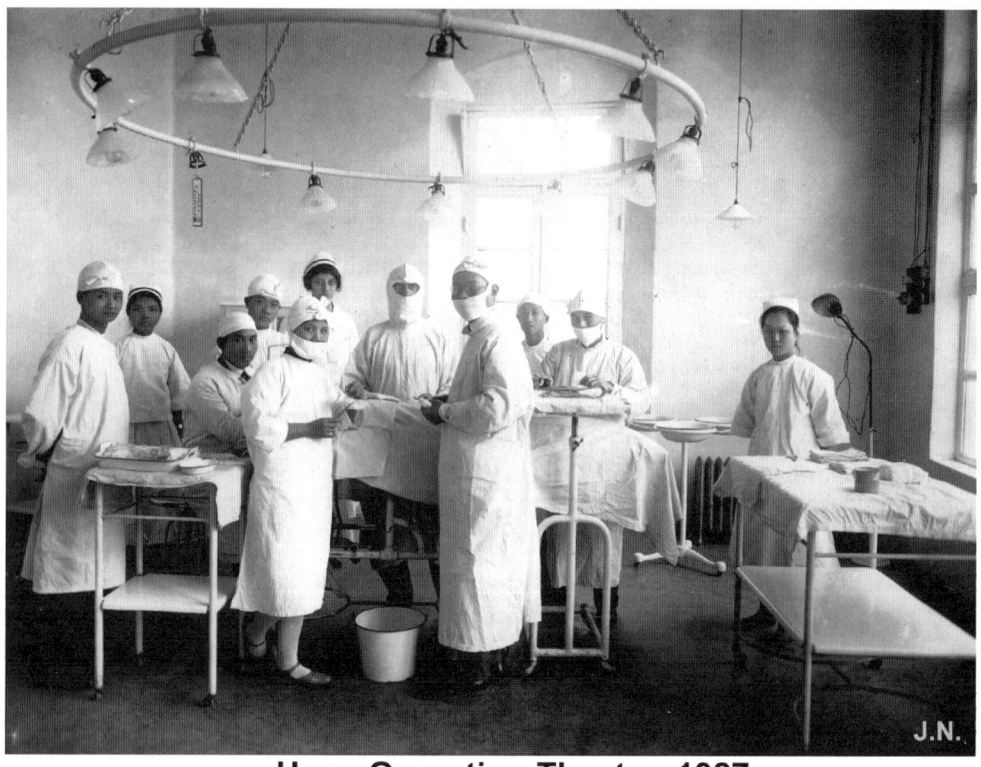

Hope Operating Theater, 1927

Old Xiamen
Cradle of Modern Chinese Business & Chinese Business Education

Chinese and Foreigners Work Together The Amoy missionaries were eventually joined in their drive for modern education by wealthy and visionary Chinese, as well as by influential foreigners like U.S. Amoy Consul Burlingame Johnson, who in 1898 started Gulangyu's prestigious Tung-Wen Institute. Although U.S. Consuls continued on as presidents of the board, the Board of Trustees was composed of the wealthy Chinese who funded not only this school but also many of the other institutes that missionaries had founded over the previous five decades. It was these 20+ institutes that led Amoy to pioneer modern China's women's education, modern sports, vocational education, arts and literature, science, aviation, oceanography, and music.

Managers of Amoy Girls' Primary and Middle Schools
Three women between Ms. Holkeboer (left) and Beekman (right) are Mrs. Sim (Joyce), who works with 800 high school boys), Dr. Chuang, obstetrician of Hope and Wilhelmina Hospital, and Miss Ho, principal of Charlotte W. Duryee Bible School.
(all alumnae)

Wealthy Xiamen Chinese Fund Modern Education Speaking of educational work in the Annual Trade Report of Amoy for 1909 the Commissioner uses these significant words: "The forward educational movement, which has made so much headway all over China, has at this port been continued with greater impetus than before. All the educational establishments report large increase in students; and the wealthy class continue to cooperate handsomely in this great work by giving large sums to the various institutions."

Annual Trade Report of Amoy, 1909

中国人和外国人一起努力 最后，有远见的中国富人和有影响力的外国人纷纷加入，共同推进中国的现代教育。其中包括美国驻厦领事巴詹声。巴詹声于1898年创办了鼓浪屿岛上著名的同文学院。尽管后任的美国领事继续担任学院理事长，但学院理事会成员中有不少富裕的中国人。他们不仅资助同文学院，同时也资助传教士在过去50多年中创办的众多其他学校。正是这20多所学校使得厦门成为开创中国现代女子教育、现代体育教育、现代职业教育、现代妇女医学、文学艺术、科学、航空航海和音乐的先驱。

厦门有钱人资助现代教育 在1909年厦门年度贸易报告中，谈到教育工作时，委员会委员使用了这些重要字眼：迅速发展的教育运动，在全中国取得了长足进步。厦门这个港口城市比以往更大的力量继续推进这项工作。所有的教育机构都报告说，学生人数大增。富裕阶层积极参与这项伟大的工程，并慷慨地向各类教育机构投入大笔资金。

——《厦门贸易年度报告》，1909年

East and West on Gulangyu (around 1900)　　Jim Cummings

Old Xiamen
Cradle of Modern Chinese Business & Chinese Business Education

Tung-Wen Institute was first established on Kolongsu about 1898 in a native house, and a building erected in 1902…The founder of this Institute was Mr. A. Burlingame Johnson, then U. S. Consul at Amoy. He enlisted the cooperation and support of a number of wealthy Chinese gentlemen, from whom a Board of Trustees was chosen and by whom the Institute has ever since been successfully conducted. By constitutional authority the resident U. S. Consul is made President of the Board, and the Commissioner of Customs Vice President.

The Outlook, 1903

Tongwen Institute, Amoy (Bowra, 1908)

Anglo-Chinese College, Amoy

同文学院 最初大约在 1898 年设立在鼓浪屿的一所居民房子里。1902 年，建设了自己的大楼。

这所学院的创始人是 A. 伯林盖姆·约翰逊，时任美国驻厦门领事。他获得了中国许多有钱人的帮助和支持，从他们中选派人员，组成了理事会，并成功地运营了这所学院。学院章程规定，常驻美国领事为理事会主席，海关关长为副主席。

——《瞭望》，1903 年

Amoy Boy Scouts, 1920s (Bruce)

Old Xiamen
Cradle of Modern Chinese Business & Chinese Business Education

"I am a daughter of Gulangyu Islet. In my dreams I often return to the shores of Gulangyu, where the sea is boundless, blue and beautiful."

Dr. Lin Qiaozhi, Mother of Modern Chinese Women's Medicine

Father of Pinyin

Education Made Amoy #1 Amoy's pioneering education, including its women's education, enabled the tiny island city to produce literally hundreds of people who influenced modern China and Asia—people like Lin Qiao Zhi, mother of modern Chinese women's medicine; John Ma, China's first modern sports coach; Lin Yutang, one of the 20th century's greatest international writers; Teng Hiok Chiu[1],(ZhouTingxu, 周廷旭), famous artist and first Chinese to win an Olympic medal; Horace Talmage Day, famous American painter born in Amoy in 1909[2]; Lu Zhuangzhang,[3] (卢戆章), 1854-1928, "Father of Pinyin"; Walter Brattain (沃尔特·布拉顿), co-recipient of the Nobel Prize for inventing the transistor; and literally hundreds of famous Chinese musicians, including Yin Chengzong (殷承宗), whom the New York Times deemed the best Chinese pianist on the planet.[4]

---

[1] While studying abroad, 21-yr-old Teng Hiok Chiu won a bronze with the British basketball team in the 1924 Paris Olympics. Rose Tang wrote Chiu "was the 1st foreign artist to win the Turner Gold Medal and the Royal Academy Gold medal for his paintings." Queen Mary attended his 1929 solo exhibition in London, and he was the first foreign Associate of the Royal Society of British Artists.

[2] Day's son, who has provided me scans of his father's letters and paintings, has shown me paintings of Amoy that his father produced when only 8 years old.

[3] Examine the granite stones as you ascend "Pinyin Path" (Gusheng Rd) from Gulangyu's beach to Anxian Hall and you'll discover many are engraved with punctuation marks, letters and Pinyin. These are an unusual but fitting tribute to Lu Zhuangzhang.

[4] Befitting an islet that produced so many great musicians, Gulangyu also has Asia's largest piano museum.

商业老厦门
现代中国商业与工商管理教育的摇篮

> 我是鼓浪屿的女儿,我常常在梦中回到鼓浪屿的大海边。那海面真辽阔,那海水真蓝,真美。
>
> ——中国现代妇产科之母林巧稚

教育造就的厦门第一 厦门在教育领域包括女子教育领域的开创性贡献,让这个小岛得以培育出数百名影响现代中国和亚洲的人物。他们包括:林巧稚,中国现代妇科医学之母;马约翰,中国现代体育的第一名教练;林语堂,20世纪世界最伟大的作家之一;周廷旭,[①]著名画家中国赢取奥林匹克奖牌第一人;贺拉斯·打马字·戴,1909年出生于厦门

Dr. Lin Qiaozhi
Mother of Modern Women's Medicine

Dr. Lin Wenqing (Lim Boon Keng)

的著名美国画家[②];卢戆章[③],"汉语拼音之父";数以百计中国著名的音乐家[④],包括被《纽约时报》誉为世界上最优秀的中国钢琴家殷承宗,以及因发明晶体管而成为诺贝尔物理学奖共同获得者沃尔特·布拉顿。

---

① 在国外留学期间,21岁的周廷旭加入英国篮球队。他们在1924年巴黎奥运会上获得铜牌。罗丝·唐写道,周廷旭是第一个因油画获得特纳金奖和皇家学院金奖的外国画家。玛丽女王参观了周廷旭1929年在伦敦举办的个展。他还是第一个入选英国艺术家皇家协会的外国人。

② 戴的儿子曾经向我提供了他父亲的信件和绘画作品,并向我展示了他父亲8岁时在画的厦门风景画。

③ 当你从沙滩沿着小路往安献堂上行时,如果留意脚底的花岗岩,你就会发现上面刻着标点符号、字母和拼音。这些有规律的雕刻是给卢戆章(1854-1928)的一份不同寻常却又恰如其分的献礼。
卢戆章是同安人,在新加坡学习英语,于1928年返回鼓浪屿定居,帮助一位英国传教士编纂《英华字典》。

④ 得益于鼓浪屿的文化及音乐遗产,鼓浪屿现在拥有亚洲最大的钢琴博物馆和世界最大的管弦博物馆。

189

Old Xiamen
Cradle of Modern Chinese Business & Chinese Business Education

From "With Love and Irony" (Lin Yutang)

John Ma, began his athletic career as a child in the playgrounds of "Fumin Elementary School (福民小学). Celebrated astronomer Yu Qingsong (余青松) and the writer Lin Yutang (林语堂) studied at Gulangyu Yangyuan Primary School (鼓浪屿养元小学). The New York Times' obituary for Lin Yutang noted:

"Lin Yutang, poet, novelist, historian and philosopher, had no peer as an interpreter to Western minds of the customs, aspirations, fears and thoughts of his people and their country, China, the great and tragic land."①

Chinese Typewriter
Lin Yutang's Invention

Lu Xun, Founder of Modern Chinese Literature

---

① "Lin Yutang, 80, Dies; Scholar-Philosopher", *New York Times*.

商业老厦门
现代中国商业与工商管理教育的摇篮

马约翰小时候在福民小学的操场上开始了他的运动生涯。著名的天文学家余青松和作家林语堂在鼓浪屿养元小学读过书。《纽约时报》在林语堂的讣告中写道：

"林语堂，诗人，小说家，历史学家，哲学家。他向西方诠释了中国这个多灾多难大国的风土人情，以及中国人的所盼、所虑和所思。在这方面，他成绩卓著，无人能比。"①

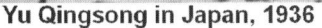
Yu Qingsong in Japan, 1936

John Ma, Father of Modern Chinese Sports

---

① 刊于1976年3月27日《纽约时报》。

Xiamen University – China's Future in the 1920s   Gulangyu's International Settlement was a great attraction for wealthy Chinese abroad who wanted to return to their homeland but were fearful of the political upheavals and war. With its own elected government, and its own police force, Gulangyu was a safe haven for foreigners and wealthy Chinese alike, who cooperated closely. But the most far-reaching contribution to Amoy's future was made by a Chinese who chose to live not safely within the international enclave of Gulangyu but in his small home village of Jimei, just across the bay.   And when Mr. Tah Kah Kee, the "Henry Ford of Asia," built Xiamen University in 1921, he did so not as a venture with foreigners but on his own.

厦门大学——20世纪20年代中国的未来　对那些想回故乡却又担心政治纷争和战争的海外富裕华人来说,鼓浪屿国际租界吸引力很大。租界有自选的自治政府和警察,对外国人和富裕的中国人来说是一个安全的避风港。在那里,他们紧密合作。但对厦门未来做出深远影响和贡献的却是一名中国人。他没有选择安全地居住在鼓浪屿国际租界里,而是住在厦门港湾对面的一个小村庄——集美。当1921年陈嘉庚这位"亚洲的亨利·福特"创办厦门大学的时候,他们没有与外国人合作投资,而是完全依靠自己。

1926年时的厦门大学全景(鲁迅先生寄与许广平先生之明信片)

Chapter 8   Xiamen University
Pioneer in Modern Chinese Business Education

XMU—90 Years of Pioneering Education   Of Amoy's many contributions to China's modern education, its crowning achievement is Xiamen University (formerly Amoy University), which has pioneered numerous fields from aviation to oceanography (see appendix). But nowhere has XMU excelled more than in economics and business education—which is no surprise, given the values and goals of XMU's entrepreneurial founder, Mr. Tan Kah Kee.

A true rags to riches story, the legendary "Henry Ford of Asia" went from working Amoy's fields and fishnets to building a business empire that by the mid 1920s had 30,000 employees in 150 offices and 48 countries. But he is best remembered, and loved, for devoting his life to the cause of education both at home and abroad.

Although history shows Amoynese have always cherished education, Tan Kah Kee took it to a new level. Mr. Tan frequently quoted his motto, "Education is a nation's foundation, its promotion the responsibility of its people," but for the visionary Tan, it was not just a motto but a lifestyle.

 At age 21, Tan Kah Kee started his first school in his Amoy hometown of Jimei Village. And thanks to both his business acumen and frugal lifestyle, he went on to donate an estimated USD $10 million (over USD $100 million in today's dollars) to start dozens of schools throughout Asia. But the apple of Tan's eye (or "bright pearl in one's palm," as Chinese put it) was Xiamen University.

第八章　厦门大学
——中国现代工商管理教育的先驱

厦大——90年兴学筚路蓝缕　在厦门对中国现代教育的诸多贡献中，最引人瞩目的成就是厦门大学（旧称为 Amoy University）。从航空学到海洋学（见附录），厦门大学已经成为无数领域的先驱。但任何领域都不如经济学和工商管理教育那样突出。这不足为奇，因为这两个学科是厦门大学的创办者陈嘉庚先生所推崇的价值和目标。

陈嘉庚，富有传奇色彩的"亚洲亨利·福特"经历了"从贫民变富翁"的真实故事。他从厦门的田间地头、海边渔村走出来，变成一个商业帝国的缔造者，至20世纪20年代中期，在48个国家设立了150个办事处，拥有雇员3万人。但是，人们纪念他，热爱他，是因为他把毕生的精力奉献给了国内外的教育事业。

历史上，厦门人一直崇尚教育。但陈嘉庚先生却将这种重视提升到一个新的高度。陈先生总是反复强调自己的座右铭："教育为立国之本，兴学乃国民天职。"对陈嘉庚来说，这个理想并不仅是一个座右铭，而是一种生活方式。

陈嘉庚21岁时便在自己的家乡集美村创办了第一所学校。得益于自己的商业天赋和生活的节俭，陈嘉庚先后捐赠大约1,000万美元（相当于现在1亿多美元），在亚洲各国兴办数十所学校。然而，被陈嘉庚先生视为掌上明珠的却是厦门大学。

XMU—China's Hope for the Future (1920) Tucked out amidst Amoy's rice fields, between the picturesque "Five Old Men Mountains" and the beach, Tan's bold venture fired the imaginations of not just Chinese but foreigners such as Paul Hutchinson. In 1920, months before the first block of Minnan granite was reverently set in place, Hutchinson wrote about the hope that XMU promised for China's future:

"This school [Xiamen University] is entirely a Chinese institution, with no foreign teachers and no foreign connections, and right out in a small Chinese village. The course of study is being made very practical… When we think of the future days, it is one of the most encouraging things to be seen in the whole of China."

Paul Hutchinson,
1920

Both a visionary and a pragmatist Tan started XMU with a teacher's college and a business college. The teacher's college was to make modern Chinese education sustainable by training new generations of academics. The business college aimed to perpetuate both modern practical knowledge as well as the vision and values behind centuries of Amoynese' success.

商业老厦门
现代中国商业与工商管理教育的摇篮

厦门大学——中国未来的希望（20 世纪 20 年代） 厦门大学位于风景如画的五老峰与海滩之间，隐藏在片片稻田之中。陈嘉庚大胆的投资激发了中国人以及诸如胡金生（Paul Hutchinson）之类的外国人的想象力。1920 年，在第一块闽南花岗岩石被虔诚地奠基之前几个月，胡金生就写下了厦门大学对中国未来所承载的希望：

> "这所学校（厦门大学）是一个名副其实的中国学校，没有外籍教师，没有海外关联，而且地处中国一个小村庄。学科设置实用性很强……想到未来，这是整个中国最令人激动人心的事情之一。"
>
> 胡金生，1920 年

理想主义者，同时也是实干家 陈嘉庚从教育学院和商学院入手创建了厦门大学。教育学院通过培养新一代的学者使中国的现代教育得以持续发展。商学院的目标是为了延续现代实用知识以及数百年来厦门人成功背后的梦想和价值。

Old Xiamen
Cradle of Modern Chinese Business & Chinese Business Education

Both Chinese and Global   Although XMU began as a Chinese university with no foreign teachers and no foreign connections, Tan's experience in dozens of countries had shown him the global nature of business on a planet that even a century ago was shrinking rapidly. He therefore adopted as one of XMU's goals, "Promote awareness of world cultures." Even Tan's unusual blend of Chinese and Western architecture—Western edifices crowned with elegant Chinese roofs—represented his vision of a modern global curriculum built upon solid Chinese values and principles.

Pen in One Hand, Gun in the Other   With its Overseas Chinese connections and support, and strategic location on the coast between Hong Kong and Shanghai, facing Taiwan, XMU rapidly gained a reputation as "The Strength of the South," attracting both Chinese and foreign scholars. But in the late 1930s, Amoy's "strategic" location showed itself to have a downside as well, and entered several decades of difficult times.

At the outbreak of the Second Sino-Japanese War in 1936, XMU relocated to the remote mountains of Western Fujian. Famed as the start of Mao's Long March, Changting seemed more like the Long Retreat as faculty and students stuck it out for eight years in makeshift facilities and a converted temple. XMU returned to its Amoy campus in 1946—just in time to bear the brunt of the mainland's strained relationship with Taiwan during the 50s and 60s. While the rest of China was at last at peace, XMU students patrolled the beach and held classes in bomb shelters, and earned the unenviable reputation of being China's only students who studied with "pen in one hand, gun in the other."

Xiamen University, 1926

商业老厦门
现代中国商业与工商管理教育的摇篮

中西合璧 作为一所中国人的大学,厦门大学在创办之初并没有任何外国教师和海外联系。但是,陈嘉庚在数十个国家的经历已经向他展示了全球商业的本质:100多年前,我们的星球已经在快速变小。因此,他把"博集东西各国之学术及其精神"作为厦大办学宗旨之一。陈嘉庚把中西方建筑巧妙地融为一体,在西式建筑之上冠以雅致的中式屋顶,体现了他的办学理想:即建立在坚实的中国价值准则之上的现代国际化教育。

萨本栋校长与部分师生
摄于长汀校门前
XMU at Changting

一手拿笔,一手持枪 得益于海外关系和华侨资助,以及战略地位(位于香港和上海之间的沿海地区,面对台湾),厦门大学迅速赢得了"南方之强"的美誉,也吸引了海内外众多学者。但是,在20世纪30年代后期,厦门大学进入数十年的困难时期,"战略"地位变成了她的劣势。

1936年,随着第二次中日战争的爆发,厦门大学迁移至闽西边远山区——长汀。长汀因是毛泽东长征的出发地而著名,而此时长汀更像"长停",因为厦大的各个院系和学生在这里的临时校舍和寺庙里坚持了8年。1946年,厦门大学回迁后,赶上了五六十年代大陆与台湾的紧张关系,并因此承受了最沉重的压力。在中国其他地区终于安享太平之时,厦大学生却在海滩上巡逻放哨,在防空洞里上课,并由此赢得了中国唯一一所大学学生"一手拿笔,一手持枪"这种无人羡慕的美誉。

薪传——长汀时期的通草菜油灯
Study by Lamplight at XMU, Changting

脂穷於为薪,火传也。
不知其尽也。——莊子
紫宫薪火断续中,
草菜油灯焚继旦。——嚴少顯诗

朱一雄绘

Old Xiamen
Cradle of Modern Chinese Business & Chinese Business Education

Strength of the Nation Yet even as centuries of Amoy's people had thrived in the face of adversity, so Amoy's university not only kept pace with the rest of China but actually led the nation in several fields, suggesting XMU was not just the "Strength of the South" but a "Strength of the Nation." During China's relative isolation of the 1950s, for example, the Overseas College started China's first correspondence program for Chinese and foreigners abroad—five decades before information technology made "distance learning" a cutting edge educational model in the rest of the world. Since the 1950s, XMU has taught over 30,000 correspondence students from over 100 countries and regions. (The school also pioneered on-campus education for foreigners in China, and now has almost 2000 foreign students studying everything from Minnan Dialect to acupuncture.)

President Zhu and President Gabriel Buget
Ecole Normale Superieure, Paris
朱校长向巴黎高师校长 **Ruget** 教授
赠送学校纪念牌

In 1952, Beijing declared XMU one of the nation's 14 comprehensive universities, and in 1963 it became a "key" university directly under the Ministry of Education. Even today, XMU is the only key university in a Special Economic Zone. With 3 campuses covering over 600 hectares, XMU has over 38,000 on-campus students, including 20,575 undergraduates, 15,590 masters students, 2,483 doctoral students, and over 2,022 students from Hong Kong, Taiwan, Macao and abroad. And the Strength of the South continues to grow, thanks to the loyal support of over 200,000 alumni at home and abroad.

Tan Kah Kee, the man who dreamed of a truly Chinese university with a global scope, would have been proud to know that the "bright pearl in his hand" now has academic ties with over 150 institutions of higher education, including universities in the UK, the USA, Canada, Japan, France, Germany, Russia, Hong Kong, Taiwan, and Macao. And being the entrepreneur that he was, he would no doubt be pleased by XMU's leadership in economics and business education.

商业老厦门
现代中国商业与工商管理教育的摇篮

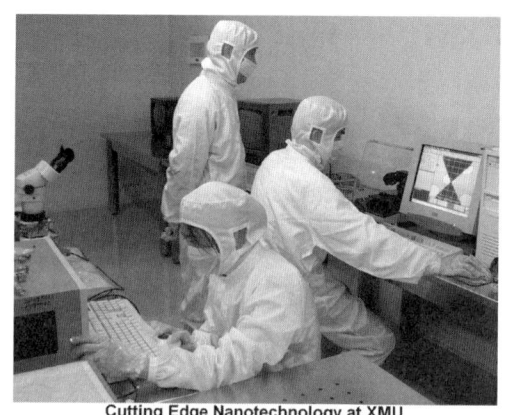
Cutting Edge Nanotechnology at XMU

中国之强 数百年来,厦门人面对逆境蓬勃发展。厦门大学也同样跟上了中国其他地区的发展步伐,并在诸多领域处于领先地位。这让人想起,厦大不仅是"南方之强",而且是"中国之强"。比如说,在中国比较封闭的20世纪50年代,厦大海外学院就为海外的中国人和外国人开办了中国第一个函授教育课程。在信息技术使"远程教育"成为世界其他国家的尖端教育模式之前,厦大海外学院已经领先了半个世纪。自20世纪50年代以来,厦门大学已经接受了来自100多个国家和地区的3万多名函授生。该学院在为外国人提供全日制教育方面也是中国领先。目前,学院拥有近2000名外国留学生,开设从闽南话到针灸等所有科目。

1952年,北京宣布厦门大学为中国14所综合性大学之一。1963年,厦大成为国家教育部直属的一所重点大学。如今,厦门大学是中国唯一一所位于经济特区的重点大学。厦门大学目前拥有三个校区,占地面积超过600公顷,在校生超过3.8万人,包括20575名本科生,15590名硕士研究生和2483名博士研究生以及来自香港、台湾、澳门和其他国家的2022名留学生。得益于海内外二十多万名校友的忠实支持,南方之强还在不断发展、壮大。

"一所拥有国际视野的真正的中国大学"是陈嘉庚先生的梦想。要是知道自己的"掌上明珠"目前已经同包括英国、美国、加拿大、日本、法国、德国、俄罗斯等国家以及中国香港、台湾和澳门等地区在内的150多所高等教育机构建立了学术联系,陈先生应该会感到自豪。作为一名企业家,他无疑会为厦大在经济学和工商管理教育领域的领先地位感到欣慰。

XMU Presents Honorary Professorship to Michael Dell

Old Xiamen
Cradle of Modern Chinese Business & Chinese Business Education

Appendix — Some of XMU's Many Firsts

China's only key university founded by an Overseas Chinese
中国唯一一所由海外华侨创办的重点大学

China's 1st Institute of higher degrees in Higher Education Research
中国第一个高等教育研究所和高等教育学位

China's only key university in a Special Economic Zone
中国经济特区中唯一一所重点大学

China's leading economics college
中国主要的经济学院

China's first economics journal (1959)
中国第一份经济刊物 (1959 年)

One of China's 1st Departments of Economics and Trade
中国最早的经贸学院之一

A "Cradle of modern aviation"
"现代航空学的摇篮"

A "Cradle of modern Chinese oceanography"
"现代中国海洋学的摇篮"

China's First PhD in Oceanography
培养了海洋学的第一个博士

China's leading chemistry department
中国实力最强的化学系

China's #1 State Key Laboratory in Physical Chemistry of Solid Surfaces
最好的中国固体表面物理化学国家 1 号重点实验室

China's only Key Laboratory in Analytical Sciences (the Materials and Life Chemistry)
中国唯一的分析科学重点实验室
(数学和生命化学)

China's 1st Taiwan Research Center
中国第一个台湾研究所

China's 1st Taiwan research quarterly)
中国第一份台湾研究刊物

China's 1st institute of S.E. Asian and Overseas Chinese Studies
中国第一个东南亚及海外华人华侨研究机构

China's 1st Anthropology Museum
中国第一个人类博物馆

China's 1st EMBA to enroll students (4th most popular E-MBA today)
中国第一次招收 EMBA 学生的大学（目前是第四大热门的 EMBA 学校）

China's largest number of enrolled EMBA students
中国招收最多 EMBA 学生的大学

China's 1st modern college for foreigners (OEC, 1950s)
中国为外国学生设立的第一所现代大学

China's pioneer in correspondence education (since 1950s!)
中国函授教育的先驱（从 20 世纪 50 年代始）

China's closest university ties with Taiwan.
中国离台湾最近的大学

One of China's 1st universities to teach International Law
中国最早教授国际法的大学之一

One of China's leaders in political affairs research
中国政治事件研究的领先者之一

Inter-university ties with at least 89 foreign institutes
至少与 89 个外国学院建立校际联系

China's most beautiful campus (only Wuhan University comes close).
中国最美丽的校园（只有武汉大学能媲美）

China's largest university auditorium (overlooking the sea)
中国最大的大学礼堂（眺望大海）

          And the list goes   此列表将继续添加…

School of Management, Xiamen University (SMXMU)

SMXMU—A Leader in Internationalization   Like its mother university, SMXMU has a long history of internationalization. As early as the 1980s, XMU became one of eight universities in China to participate in the China-Canada Management Education Program (CCMEP). Between 1983 and 1992, XMU sent over 70 faculty members to Canadian universities' business Schools for research, as visiting scholars, or to complete a degree program. Afterwards, they returned to revolutionize XMU business education with their newly learned course structure, advanced teaching methodology and modern textbooks.

In 1986, XMU and two Canadian universities, Dalhousie and Saint Mary's, jointly launched the MBA Education Centre, and in 1987, recruited the first business administration masters students.

In 1991, XMU became one of China's first nine universities to recruit MBA students, and in 2002 it became one of China's pioneers in EMBA education.

Dean Shen Yifeng, Berlin, 2010

Since 2006, the School of Management has sent 27 MBA/EMBA faculty members to Harvard Business School to participate in "Program on Case Method and Participant-Centered Learning (PCMPCL)" and "Global Colloquium on Participant-Centered Learning," and in 2007, SMXMU co-hosted Harvard Business School's CWCD program. The School also has student exchanges with such universities as Kellogg School of Management, Northwestern University, Southampton University, McGill University, and the German universities of Trier and Furtwangen.

厦门大学管理学院

厦门大学管理学院——国际化的领导者 与她的母体一样,厦大管理学院也拥有国际化的悠久历史。早在20世纪80年代,厦门大学就是中国八所参与中加管理教育交流项目(CCMEP)

的高校之一。1983年至1992年,厦大先后派出70多名教师前往加拿大各大学商学院留学、进修或研究。他们学成归来后,利用自己新学的课程设置、先进的教学方法和现代的教科书籍,改革厦大工商管理教育。

1986年,厦门大学与加拿大两所大学——达尔豪西和圣玛丽联手创办了工商管理教育中心,并于1987年联合招收第一批工商管理硕士研究生。

1991年,厦门大学成为中国首批九所招收MBA研究生的大学之一。

2002年,又成为中国开展EMBA教育的先锋之一。

2006年以来,管理学院已经向哈佛商学院派出了27名MBA和EMBA教师,参加"个案教学法(PCMPCL)"和"以学生为中心的案例教学法(GCPCL)"等进修课程。2007年,厦门大学管理学院与哈佛商学院联合主办了"案例写作与课程开发"(CWCD)培训项目。学院与诸如美国西北大学凯洛格商学院、英国南安普敦大学、加拿大麦吉尔大学以及德国的特里尔和富特旺根等大学开展交换生项目。

Old Xiamen
Cradle of Modern Chinese Business & Chinese Business Education

Today, SMXMU has over 6,000 on-campus students, including 1,800 undergraduates, 4,000+ masters students and 153 doctoral students, and is known for having China's best programs in accounting, banking and finance.

First in Accounting, Finance and Banking   SMXMU had China's first PhD programs in accounting, in management accounting, and in auditing, and has graduated almost 1/3 of all of China's accounting PhDs. SMXMU also gave the first PhD in China for a foreigner in accounting. The School is also famed as "The Cradle for CFOs," with fully 1/3 of MBA alumni working in finance, accounting and banking.

Global Honors for SMXMU include:

2006: ***BusinessWeek's*** "Top Business School List"

2007: ***Forbes & BusinessWeek's*** Only top ten MBA and EMBA outside Beijing and Shangxhai

2005, 2009: ***Forbes*** only Top Ten MBA and EMBA Programs not in Beijing or Shanghai Areas

2010: ***Forbes'*** #9 Full-time MBA in China, #10 Part-Time MBA in China, #9 in "China's Most Valued VEMBA Programmes"

如今，厦门大学管理学院拥有 6,000 多名在校生，包括 1,800 名本科生，4,000 多名硕士研究生和 153 名博士研究生。学院拥有被公认为中国最好的会计学、财务学等课程。

厦门大学管理学院开设了中国第一个会计学、财务管理和审计学博士研究生课程，拥有中国近三分之一的会计学博士生。学院还首次在中国将会计学博士学位授予一名外国人。厦门大学管理学院以"首席财务官的摇篮"而著称，超过三分之一的 MBA 毕业生在财务、会计和金融等领域工作。

厦门大学管理学院获得的全球荣誉：

2006 年：上榜《商业周刊》全球最佳商学院名录；

2007 年：上榜《福布斯》和《商业周刊》评选的中国十佳 MBA 及 EMBA 学院（北京、上海之外唯一入选的学院）。

2005 年及 2009 年：上榜《福布斯》评选的中国十佳 MBA 及 EMBA 学院（北京、上海之外唯一入选的学院）。

2010 年：在《福布斯》评选的"中国最具价值全日制 MBA"中排名第九，在"中国最具价值在职 MBA"中排名第十，在中国最具价值的 EMBA 课程中排名第九。

An MBA Pays Off at SMXMU   Thanks to SMXMU's growing reputation for quality education, her graduates are a hot commodity for corporate recruiters. A full-time MBA grad's salary 5 years after graduation averages 3.4X their pre-admission salary; graduates of the part-time MBA program average 2.7X their pre-admission salary. Only 10.6% of grads were directors or senior managers before MBA study, compared with 17.7% only one year after graduation. By 2009: fully 34.6% of all XMU MBA graduates held senior management positions. Of course, SMXMU's successes don't just drop in their lap.

SMXMU Matches Grads with Employers   SMXMU graduates excel for two reasons. 1) a reputation for quality programs and accepting only the best applicants (in 2009/2010, the School had 1107 applicants apply for the MBA program's 250 positions). And 2) SMXMU is superb at matching graduates with prospective employers.

From admission to graduation, the Student Career Development Centre offers guidance, consultations, EMBA and MBA alumni job fairs, and innovative programs like the "Corporate E-Pass" Internship and Career Program. A job market information database provides students with a full corporate recruitment calendar, and recommends graduates to targeted employers. Monthly activities allow students to meet face to face with experienced senior managers who have been invited to act as career advisors.   The SMXMU Student Employment White Paper, issued each July, is an extensive compilation of the year's graduate information and a comprehensive analysis of employment prospects.

厦大管理学院MBA物有所值　　厦门大学管理学院的MBA教学质量享誉海内外，学院的毕业生已经成为猎头公司的热门对象。全日制MBA毕业五年后，其平均薪金是其入学前的3.4倍，在职MBA毕业后薪金为入学前的2.7倍。在进入厦大管理学院学习之前担任经理或高级管理人员仅占10.6%，毕业后仅一年这个比例上升至17.7%。截至2009年，有34.6%的厦大MBA毕业生担任高级管理职务。当然，厦门大学管理学院的成功并非轻而易举。

厦门大学管理学院为毕业生和用人单位做媒　　厦门大学管理学院毕业生之所以优秀，有两个原因：（1）教学质量声誉好并且只招收最好的学生（2009/2010年度，学院收到1107份申请，争夺250个MBA名额）；（2）在为毕业生寻找潜在的用人单位方面，学院堪称一流。

从入学到毕业，学院的职业发展中心向学生提供咨询、指导服务，创办EMBA暨MBA校友人才集市，并开设诸如"企业E-Pass"见习和职业规划等创新型课程。学院拥有用人单位的信息资料库，专门研究人才市场，向毕业生全方位提供公司招聘等信息，并把毕业生推荐给目标客户。

学院每月举办各种活动，让学生有机会面对面接触经验丰富的高级管理人员，让他们充当学生的职业规划顾问。

《厦门大学管理学院毕业生就业白皮书》每年7月发布，全面收录了本年度毕业生的个人信息，并对就业形势进行深入的分析。

Old Xiamen
Cradle of Modern Chinese Business & Chinese Business Education

International Students' Career Development is also a growing focus for SMXMU. In the past, most graduating international students returned home or enrolled in higher academic programs, but given the growing number of foreign graduates seeking employment in China, the Student Career Development Centre has started to:

1. Provide employment information on firms in China, with emphasis on multinational corporations;
2. Establish liaisons with international alumni (the first step in developing an international alumni network);
3. Build "hand-in-hand" peer support relationships between Chinese and international students to help international students overcome the language and culture barriers that may hinder their job prospects.

国际学生的职业发展　　也越来越成为厦门大学管理学院关注的焦点。过去,留学生毕业后大多返回自己的国家或选择继续深造。由于越来越多的留学生在中国谋求职业,学院的职业发展中心现在已经开始:

1. 为国际留学生提供中国公司,特别是跨国公司的招聘信息;
2. 与国际校友建立联系,目的是为了最终建立国际校友网络;
3. 在中国学生与留学生之间建立"手拉手"互助关系,帮助留学生克服可能影响其职业前途的语言和文化障碍。

Old Xiamen
Cradle of Modern Chinese Business & Chinese Business Education

Growing Alumni Network Xiamen University has long been known for its intensely loyal base of successful alumni—people like Ms. Cai Shiyue (蔡悦诗, Sarinthorn Sriyuksiri), an industrialist from Thailand, and her husband Dean Zhengzeng (丁政曾), also an XMU alumnus. She provided the funds for XMU's towering 21 storey "Song'en" Building, and the adjacent Jianwen Building. At XMU's 80th anniversary, Ms. Cai Shiyue joked that the A and B students return to XMU as professors but the C and D students go into business and donate the money to build more buildings for their university.

These alumni have contributed generously to not only XMU but also the School of Management. SMXMU's Baoxin Liying Building, for example, was built by XMU alumnus Mr. Huang Baoxin (黄保欣), former Vice Chairman of the Committee for the Basic Law of the HKSAR, and his wife Ms. Wu Liying (吴丽英), also an XMU alumnus. But SMXMU now has its own growing body of almost 20,000 fiercely loyal and generous alumni committed to the School's continuous advance.

商业老厦门
现代中国商业与工商管理教育的摇篮

不断发展的校友网络 长期以来,厦门大学以其成功校友的高度忠诚而著称。这其中包括泰国实业家蔡悦诗女士和她的丈夫、厦大校友丁政曾等。蔡女士捐资兴建了厦门大学21层高的颂恩楼和旁边的建文楼。在厦门大学建校80周年纪念会上,

蔡女士开玩笑说,A同学和B同学回到厦大当教授,C同学和D同学下海经商并捐资为自己的母校兴建更多的楼房。

这些校友慷慨捐资的对象不仅仅是厦门大学,也包括管理学院。例如,保欣丽英楼就是由原香港特别行政区基本法委员会副主席、厦大校友黄保欣先生和他的妻子、厦大校友吴丽英女士捐建的。如今,管理学院已经拥有近两万极度忠诚、慷慨的校友。他们对学院的持续发展做出了贡献。

Old Xiamen
Cradle of Modern Chinese Business & Chinese Business Education

SMXMU's list of alumni reads like a Who's Who of Chinese Business, and includes:

The president of Bank of China, the chairman of the board of China Minsheng Banking Group., Ltd., the chairman of the board of Industrial Bank Co., Ltd., the chairman of the board of UnionPay, the chairman of the board of Guotai Junan Securities Co., Ltd., vice-president of China Securities Regulatory Commission, the chairman of the board of Haitong Securities Co., Ltd., the chairman of the board of Bank of Beijing, the president of Bank of China of Beijing Branch, the president of Bank of China of Zhejiang Branch, the president of Bank of China Fujian Branch, the president of Industrial and Commercial Bank of China Shanghai Branch, the president of Industrial Securities, the vice general manager of Shenzhen Stock Exchange, the chairman of the board of Xiamen Bank, etc.

These 20,000 alumni keep in close contact with their alma mater, and not only donate generously to the School's improvement but also take an active part in counseling, and even employing, SMXMU's students.

厦门大学管理学院的校友录看上去像一本《中国商界名人录》，包括：

中国银行行长，中国民生银行集团有限公司董事会主席，中国建设银行有限公司董事会主席，中国银联董事会主席，国泰君安证券公司董事会主席，中国证券管理委员会副主席，海通证券有限公司董事会主席，北京银行董事会主席，中国银行北京市分行行长，中国银行浙江省分行行长，中国银行福建省分行行长，中国工商银行上海市分行行长，兴业证券有限公司总经理，深圳证券交易所副总经理，厦门银行董事会主席等。

两万多名校友密切联系，慷慨资助厦门大学管理学院继续发展，并为学院的毕业生提供就业咨询和工作岗位。

Old Xiamen
Cradle of Modern Chinese Business & Chinese Business Education

The Future of China and Xiamen

Right Attitude to Life "Fukien has taught me how to live. Material things can be acquired anywhere in this material world, but an attitude to life can only be mastered in the right environment. Fukien provided such an environment for me."

Ch'en Sze-ching, Fukien, Christian University graduate, 1926

Book or Bird?   I long wondered if the fountain, designed by XMU's own Li Weisi (李维祀), was supposed to be an open book or a flying bird; it turns out the sculpture is both bird and book. The "Bird Book" (鸟书) fountain symbolizes "knowledge and faith flying into the future."

"Flying into the Future" (XMU's 'Bird-book Sculpture')

Winston Churchill said that the further back one can look, the further ahead one can see. It is therefore no surprise that Amoy, and Amoy University, have such bright prospects for the future, because they stand upon the shoulders of giants—although in their own day, those "giants" probably appeared no different from the other Chinese laborers slogging it out in fields and factories far from home. But then as now, appearances can be deceiving—especially in Amoy. Consider Ms. Yangying (杨英女士).

216

中国和厦门的未来

对待生活的正确态度　"福建教会了我如何去生活。在这个现实的世界里,物质的东西随处可取,但对待生活的态度只能在合适的环境中养成。福建给我提供了这样的一个环境。"

——陈哲清,福建协和大学毕业生,1926年

是书还是鸟?　一直以来,我都疑惑不解:由厦大自己的教授李维祀设计的雕塑应该是一本摊开的书还是一只翱翔的鸟?原来,它既是书也是鸟!这个鸟书喷泉象征着"飞向未来的知识和信念"。

温斯顿·丘吉尔曾经说过,一个人可以往后回顾,也可以向前观望。因此,我们说厦门和厦门大学的未来是光明的,这不足为奇,因为他们站在巨人的肩膀上,尽管在这个时候对观察家来说,这些巨人可能看上去跟在田间劳作的中国农民或工厂里干活的劳工没有什么区别。不过,现在看来,外表是富有欺骗性的,特别是在厦门。杨英女士就是一个例子。

Old Xiamen
Cradle of Modern Chinese Business & Chinese Business Education

Maid to Millionaire In 1982, a 19-year-old farm girl with all of four years' education borrowed 30 Yuan so she could buy new clothes and a bus ticket to Xiamen, where she hoped to land a job as a maid and earn 20 Yuan a month, half of which she planned to send home. Ms. Yangying did become a maid for a Xiamen University professor, but within two decades she worked her way up from maid to selling fish on the street side to becoming one of China's most innovative business women. When I interviewed her in her home, she still had a touch of her farm girl shyness, but she also showed an unshakable confidence—in herself, and in China. She said, "The whole world is coming to China, so why should we seek our fortune abroad? I made my fortune in China, and I'll continue to invest my money here at home." She then added, with a smile that betrayed some of the sagacity behind the shyness, "Besides, I'm Chinese, so I know the market here!"

Ms. Yangying's investments range from real estate development in Xiamen and Beijing to her Amoytop Biotechnology Company. But like so many Amoynese before her, she has a heart for education, and is working to help others have the schooling that she was denied.[1] She started both the Xiamen's Yingcai School and the WASC[2]-accredited Xiamen International School, and has earmarked over 300 million Yuan to build 1000 schools with Project Hope.

Ms. Yang Ying is living proof that Amoynese' vision is as farsighted as ever!

Read more about Ms. Yang Ying and other modern Amoy successes at: www.amoymagic.com/success.htm

---

[1] Ms. Yangying may only have 4 years of formal schooling, but she has at least a doctorate in the School of Life.

[2] WASC: Western Association of Schools and Colleges—one of the U.S.'s leading accreditation agencies

从保姆到百万富婆 1982年,19岁的农村姑娘杨英在读完小学4年之后,带着借来的30元,买了一套新衣服和一张前往厦门的车票,希望在厦门找到一份保姆的工作,每个月赚20元,并把其中的一半寄回老家。杨英果真成了厦门大学一位教授家里的保姆,然后在20年之内一直不断努力,从保姆变成街边卖鱼的小商贩,最后成为中国最有创新精神的女商人之一。当我在她家里采访她的时候,她似乎还保持着乡村姑娘的几分羞涩。不过,表象是富有欺骗性的,特别是在厦门。她对自己,对中国拥有一份无法动摇的信心。她说:"整个世界都来到中国,我们为什么要跑到国外去赚钱?我是在中国发的财,因此,我将继续把钱投在国内。"然后,她笑着(这种微笑透露出羞涩背后的某种睿智)又说:"还有,我是中国人,我了解这里的市场。"

杨英女士的投资范围涵括在厦门和北京的房地产开发和她的厦门特宝生物工程公司。跟先前的许多厦门人一样,她热心教育事业,努力帮助其他人完成她自己被迫放弃的学校教育。[①] 她创办了厦门英才学校和经美国西部各州高等学校协会(WASC[②])认证的厦门国际学校,并计划捐款3亿元,兴建1000所希望小学。

Celebrate Chinese Holidays
(Xiamen Int'l School Dragon Dancers)

杨英女士的事迹生动地证明了,现在的厦门人跟他们的祖先一样富有远见!

有关杨英女士的故事及其他现代厦门成功人士的故事,请登录:
http://www.amoymagic.com/success.htm

---

① 虽然杨英女士只读过四年的书,但她至少拥有社会大学的博士水平。
② WASC:美国西部各州高等学校协会,美国主要的认证机构之一。

Old Xiamen
Cradle of Modern Chinese Business & Chinese Business Education

Afterword: Two Decades [+]

I came to XMU in 1988 expecting to teach, but like Ch'en Sze-ching and his 1920s contemporary Bertrand Russell, after witnessing two decades of Xiamen's transformation firsthand, and devouring hundreds of historic documents about Amoy, I too have learned much from Xiamen not only about business but about life—and balance!

When our family disembarked the overnight boat from Hong Kong in 1988, it was hard to believe the dusty little town of Xiamen, with a skyline barely breaking the waterline, had once been the great economic and cultural powerhouse known as Amoy. But within one decade, Xiamen was transformed, and most remarkably, it had not only been #1 in economic growth but also #2 in environmental protection.

Xiamen's amazing balancing act was not a surprise to me, because like Minnanese over the past few centuries, modern Xiamen people love both business and life—and somehow manage to get the best of both. When Xiamen won the gold at the 2002 Livcom [①] competition in Stuttgart, Germany, one of the six international judges remarked, "I had no idea China had cities like this."

I hope that this booklet has helped you appreciate why most of my books on Fujian have the word "magic" in the title, because Xiamen and XMU are indeed magical.

Enjoy Amoy!

    Enjoy XMU!

    Dr. Bill Brown
    SMXMU

[①] Livcom: International Award for Livable Communities, or "The Green Oscar"; www.livcomawards.com

后记：居厦二十余载

1988年我来到厦大，希望在这里教书。跟陈哲清和同处20世纪20年代的伯特兰·罗素一样，在亲眼目睹厦门20多年的巨变，并一口气读完数百本有关厦门的历史文献之后，我自己也从厦门这里学到了许多，不仅仅是有关生意，还包括生活，以及生意与生活之间的平衡！

1988年，当我们全家人走下香港客轮、登陆厦门的时候，这里没有什么高楼，很难相信这座满是灰尘的小城就是历史上曾经被称为伟大的经济和文化的发源地。但是，在十年之间，厦门发生了巨变。最显著的是，有一段时间，厦门的经济发展速度位居全国第一，环境保护紧跟其次。

厦门令人惊奇的均衡发展并没有让人感到吃惊，因为跟先前数百年来居住厦门或遍布全球各地的闽南企业家一样，现代厦门人热衷于商业，也同时热爱生活，而且有办法在两者之间取得最佳平衡。当2002年厦门在德国斯图加特荣获"国际宜居城市金奖[①]"的时候，在六名国际评委中，有一位评委评论说："我没想到中国拥有厦门这样的城市。"

我希望这本书已经帮助你理解为什么我所撰写的有关福建的书籍名称里大多拥有"魅力"这个单词，因为厦门和厦门大学实在太神奇了。

爱我厦门！

　　爱我厦门大学！

潘维廉博士
于厦门大学管理学院

[①] Livcom："国际宜居城市金奖"，或称"宜居社区的奥斯卡"。网址：www.livcomawards.com

The Foreign "Expert" in China: Teacher or Learner?
Excerpt from, *The Problem of China*, by Bertrand Russell, 1922

"When I went to China, I went to teach; but every day that I stayed I thought less and less of what I had to teach them and more of what I had to learn from them. Among Europeans who lived a long time in China, I found this attitude not uncommon, but among those whose stay is short, or who go only to make money, it is sadly rare. It is rare because the Chinese do not excel in the things we really value— military prowess and industrial enterprise. But those who value wisdom or beauty, or even the simple enjoyment of life, will find more of these things in China than in the distracted and turbulent West, and will be happy to live where such things are valued. I wish I could hope that China, in return for our scientific knowledge, may give us something of her large tolerance and contemplative peace of mind....

"Should our lives be spent in building a mansion that we shall never have the leisure to inhabit?"

外国"专家"在中国:老师还是学生?①
(摘自《中国问题》,伯特兰·罗素著,1922年)

我当初来中国是为了教书的,但在中国停留的时间越久,我就越不知道我能教他们些什么,相反我倒是在想我能向他们学些什么。我发现,长时间在中国生活的人往往都会这么想。但对于那些只在中国生活了较短时间,或者来中国纯粹为了赚钱的人,持这种态度的人少得可怜。这是因为在我们真正重视的东西上中国无法超过我们——军事力量和经济繁荣。但是对于那些崇尚智慧或美感,甚至只是追求更高生活品味的人,他们可以在中国更多地找到他们所真正需要的东西。而这些,是他们在纷乱繁杂的西方社会所很难找到的。他们可以在中国过上幸福的生活,因为这些东西也是中国人所看重和需要的。我多么希望,中国可以给予我们她的宽容、博大、平和,就像我们在科学技术方面所给予中国的。

我们穷尽一生的时间来积聚我们永远也不会去消费的金钱值得吗?

---

① 谭倩倩译。

Other Books by Bill Brown

Magic Xiamen, XMUP (Chinese and English Versions)
《魅力厦门》，厦门大学出版社，中文版和英文版

Discover Gulangyu, XMUP (bilingual)
《魅力鼓浪屿》，厦门大学出版社，汉英对照

Old Gulangyu in Foreigners' Eyes, XMUP (bilingual)
《老外看老鼓浪屿》，厦门大学出版社，汉英对照

Xiamen University—Strength of the Nation, XMUP (bilingual)
《魅力厦门大学—中华之强》，厦门大学出版社，汉英对照

Discover Quanzhou, XMUP (bilingual)
《魅力泉州》，厦门大学出版社，汉英对照

Magic Fujian, XMUP (bilingual, and MP3 CD)
《老外看福建》，厦门大学出版社，汉英对照，配 CD
6
The Fujian Adventure, Lujiang Press (English)
《魅力福建》，鹭江出版社，英文版

The Fujian Adventure, Straits Press (Chinese)
《魅力福建》，海峡出版社，中文版

Organizational Behavior, Jiangxi People's Press (Chinese)
《组织行为学》，江西人民出版社，中文版

The Art of Business Warfare, Beijing University Press (Chinese)
《企业兵法》，北京大学出版社，中文版

Website: www.amoymagic.com

Bibliography

Abend, Hallett, "Treaty Ports," Doubleday, Doran and Company, Inc, New York, 1944

Allom, Thomas and Wright, the Reverend G.N., "China in a Series of Views, Displaying the Scenery, Architecture, and Social Habits of that Ancient Empire," Fisher, London and Paris, 1843.

The Amoy Gazette (厦门钞报)

"Amoy General Geographical Description, &c." China Review, Vol. 22, No.3, 1896

Anderson, John L., "Our Horse Races in China," in Outing, Vol. XVI, Issue 5, 5 August, 1890

Anderson, John A., M.D., "The Opium Question: A New Opportunity," in Chinese Recorder, Vol. 37, August, 1906.

Anti-Cobweb Society, "Fukien Arts and Industries: Papers by Members of the Anti-Cobweb Society, Foochow, Fukien, China," Christian Herald Industrial Press, Foochow 1933.

"Greetings from Amoy; Amoy Mission, 1842-1907," Pamphlet by Reformed Church of America.

"Asia Journal and Monthly Register for British India and its Dependencies,"; Supplementary Intelligence, Vol. XXVI, July to December 1828, London, 1828

Baldwin, Rev. S.L.D.D., "Lieutenant Wood on Missionaries in China," Chinese Recorder, Vol. 20, Nov. 1889.

Band, Edward, "Working His Purpose Out: The History of the English Presbyterian Mission," Presbyterian Church of England, London, 1948

Barbour, George F., "China and the Missions at Amoy, with Notice of the Opium Trade," William P. Kennedy, Edinburgh, 1855.

Bedloe, Edward, M.D., U.S. Consul, reporting in "Weekly Abstract of Sanitary Reports," Supervising Surgeon-General M.H,S., Government Printing Office, Washington, 1893

Bedloe, Edward, M.D., U.S. Consul in Amoy, :"Public Health Reports, Vol. 2, January 1, 1881

Blakeslee, George H., Editor, "China and the Far East: Clark University Lectures," Thomay Y. Crowell and Co., New York, 1910

Bowra, Cecil A.V., Commissioner of Customs, "Amoy," in Wright, 1908

Carles, William Le Gendre, U.S. Consul in Amoy, "How to Deal with China. A Letter to de B. Rand. Kiem, Esquire, Agent of the United States, Amoy, 1871.

Chater, Paul Cachik; Orange, James, "The Chater Collection: Pictures Relating to China, Hongkong, Macao, 1655-1860; with Historical and Descriptive Letterpress by James Orange," London, Thornton Butterworth Limited, 1924

Gordon-Cumming, Miss, "The Explosion at Amoy," St. James' Gazette, in Littell's Living Age, Feb. 4, 1888.

Cunynghame, Colonel Arthur Augustus Thurlow, "An Aide-De-Camp's Recollections of Service in China, A Residence in Hong-Kong, and Visits to Other Islands in the Chinese Seas," London, 1853

De Jong, Gerald F., "The Reformed Church in China 1842-1951," Wm. B. Eerdmans Publishing Co., Michigan, 1992

Denby, Hon. Charles, LL.D., [Thirteen Years United States Minister to China], "China and Her People: Being the Observations, Reminiscences, and Conclusions of an American Diplomat, Vol. II, L.C. Page and Company, Boston, 1906

Denby, Hon. Charles, LL.D., "China's Open Door," Lothrop Publishing, Boston, 1900

DeVelder, Walter, "A Missionary Journey Over Nine Decades" (unpublished).

Dobell, Peter, "Travels in Kamtchatka and Siberia, with a Narrative of a Residence in China, Vol. II, London, 1830. Dobell: Counselor of the Court of His Imperial Majesty the Emperor of Russia".

du Halde, P., " The General History of China," (4 vols: London, 1741), vol.1 p.169.

Dukes, Edwin Joshua, "Everyday Life in China; or, Scenes Along River and Road in Fuh-Kien," London Missionary Society's Edition, The Religious Tract Society,

56, Paternoster Row; 65, St. Paul's Churchyard; and 164, Piccadilly, 1885

Duryea, Rev. William Rankin Duryea, D.D., "The Amoy Mission," Excerpted from "A Manual of the Missions of the Reformed (Dutch) Church in America," by Sangster, Mrs. Margaret E., Ed.; Board of Publication of the Reformed Church in America, New York, 1877, pp.170-209

Edkins, Jane Rowbotham Stobbs, "Chinese Scenes and People: With Notices of Christian Missions and Missionary Life in a Series of Letters from Various Parts of China," James Nisbit and Company, London, 1863

Giles, Herbert Allan, L.L.D., "A Short History of Koolangsu," Amoy, 1878.

Goodrich, Joseph King, "The Coming China," A.C. McClure Co., Chicago, 1911

Gordon-Cumming, Miss, in "Littell's Living Age," Fifth Series, Volume LXL, No Feb. 4, 1888.

Gottschall, Terrell D., "By order of the Kaiser," Naval Institute Press, Annapolis, Maryland, 2003

Graves, Rev. Rosewell Hobart, "Forty Years in China," R.H. Woodward Company, Baltimore, 1895.

Gutzlaff, Karl F. A., "Journal of Three Voyages Along the Coast of China in 1831, 1832, and 1833," Frederick Westley and A.H. Davis, London, 1834.

Gutzlaff, Charles, Rev. by Rev. Andrew Reed, D.D., "China Opened; or, A Display of the Topography, History, Customs, Manners, Arts, Manufactures, Commerce, Literature, Religion, Jurisprudence, etc. of the Chinese Empire, Vol. II Smith, Elder & Co., London, 1838.

Haffner, Christopher, "Amoy—The Port and the Lodge," The Corinthian Lodge of Amoy, No. 1806 EC, Hong Kong, 1997

Hewlett, Sir Meyrick, "Forty Years in China," Macmillan & Co., Ltd., 1943.

Holkeboer, Tena, "God's Bridge, or the Story of Jin-Gi," Wm. B. Eerdmans Publishing Company, Grand Rapids, MI, 1944

Hughes, George, [Commissioner of Imperial Maritime Customs at Amoy] "Amoy and Surrounding Districts," De Souza and Company, Hong Kong, 1872

Hurlbut, Floy, "The Fukienese: a Study in Human Geography," Doctoral dissertation for University of Nebraska, 1939

Johnston, Rev. James., "China and Formosa; The Story of a Successful Mission," Hazell, Watson, & Viney, Ld. London, 1898

Johnston, Meta and Lena, Jin Ko-Niu—A Brief Sketch of the Life of Jessie M. Johnston For Eighteen Years W.M.A. Missionary in Amoy, China, T. French Downie 21 Warwick Lane, London, E.C. 1907

Knollys, Major Henry, "English Life in China," Smith, Elder & Company, London, 1885

Lewis, Elizabeth Foreman, "Portraits from a Chinese Scroll," the John C. Winston Company, Chicago, 1938

Little, Archibald, Mrs. "Intimate China: The Chinese as I Have Seen Them," Hutchinson & Co., London, 1899

Lowrie, Rev. Walter M., "Memoirs," Board of Foreign Missions of the Presbyterian Church, New York, 1850.

MacGowan, John, "The History of Self-Support in the London Mission," Chinese Recorder, Vol. 18, December, 1887.

Macgowan, Rev. John, "Christ or Confucius, Which?, or, The Story of the Amoy Mission," London Missionary Society, 14 Blomfield Street, E.C.; John Snow & Co., 2 Ivy Lane, Paternoster Row, E.C. 1895

Macgowan, Rev. John, "Pictures of Southern China," The Religious Tract Society, London, 1897

Macgowan, Rev. John, "Sidelights on Chinese Life," Kegan Paul, Trench, Trubner & Co., Limited, London, 1907

Macgowan, Rev. John, "Lights and Shadows of Chinese Life," North China Daily News & Herald Ltd., Shanghai, 1909

Macgowan, Rev. John, "Men and Manners of Modern China," T. Fisher Unwin, London, 1912.

Macgowan, John, "How England Saved China," T. Fisher Unwin, London, 1913.

Macgowan, John, "Beside the Bamboo," London Missionary Society, 16 New Bridge Street, London, 1914.

Macgregor, Rev. W. Letter dated January 14, 1875, in The Messenger and Missionary Record of the Presbyterian Church in England, London, April 1, 1875

Mackenzie-Grieve, Averil, "A Race of Green Ginger," Putnam, London, 1959

Maclay, Rev. R. S., "Life Among the Chinese: With Characteristic Sketches and incidents of Missionary Operations and Prospects in China," Carlton & Porter, New York, 1861.

MacPherson, D., M.D., "Two Years in China: Narrative of the Chinese Expedition, from its formation in April, 1840, to the treaty of peace in August, 1842," Saunders and Otley, London, 1843.

Manson-Bahr, Sir Philip, "Patrick Manson, The Father of Tropical Medicine," Thomas Nelson and Sons, Ltd., Edinburgh, 1962

Mayers, Wm. Fred, and Dennys, N.B., "The Treaty Ports of China and Japan," Trubner & Company, London, 1867

Metcalf, Franklin P., "Travellers and Explorers in Fukien before 1700," The Hong Kong Naturalist, December, 1934

Neill, Desmond, "Elegant Flower—First Steps in China," John Murray, Albemarle St., London, 1956

Nevius, Helen S.C., "Our Life in China," Robert Carter and Brothers, New York, 1869.

Nevius, Dr. John L., Chinese Recorder, Vol. 23, Nov. 1892.

Ng, Chin-Keong, "Trade and Society—The Amoy Network on the China Coast 1683-1735," Singapore University Press, Singapore, 1983

Oldham, Rev. H.W., "Educational Mission Work in and near Amoy," Changpu, in Chinese Recorder, June 1908.

Orange, James, :The Chater Collection; Pictures Relating to China, Hongkong, Macao, 1865-1860, Thornton Butterworth, Limited, London, 1924

Pitcher, Philip Wilson, "Fifty Years in Amoy, a History of the Amoy Mission," Reformed Church of America Board of Publication, NY, 1893

Pitcher, Philip Wilson, "In and About Amoy," Methodist Publishing House, Shanghai, 1912

Sadler, Rev. James F., "The Anglo-Chinese College at Amoy," in Gaunt, 1899.

Sangster, Mrs. Margaret E., Ed.; "A Manual of the Missions of the Reformed (Dutch) Church in America," Board of Publication of the Reformed Church in America, New York, 1877.
Scott, Roderick, "Fukien Christian University," United Board for Christian Colleges in China, NY, 1954.

Selby, Thomas Gunn, "As the Chinese See Us," Fisher Unwin, London, 1901

Shore, Hon. Henry Noel, R.N., "The Flight of the Lapwing, A Naval Officer's Jottings in China, Formosa and Japan," Longmans, Green and Company, London, 1881

Smith, D. Warres, "European Settlements in the Far East," Sampson, Low, Marston & Company, London, 1900

Smith, Mary Augusta Doty, "The China Story: Recollections of a Little Girl's Life in Amoy, China," unpublished memoir. [Daughter of Elihu Doty, RCA Missionary to China, 1844-1864]

Smith, Rev. J.N.B., "Money and Missions, in Chinese Recorder, Vol. 29, No. 2, Feb. 1898

Smith, George, A Narrative of an Exploratory Visit to Each of the Consular Cities of China, on behalf of the Church Missionary Society, in the Years 1844, 1845, 1846," Harper and Brothers Publishers, New York, 1857.

Soothill, William E., "A Mission in China," Young People's Missionary Movement, New York, 1907

Stoddard, John L., "Stoddard's Lectures," Stationer's Hall, London, 1897

Surgeon T.T. Jeans, R.N., "Badminton Magazine of Sports and Pastimes, Vol. V, July to Dec. 1897"

Tai, En Sai, "Treaty Ports in China: a Study in Diplomacy," Columbia University Printing Office, New York, 1918

Talman, Rose H., "Our China Years, 1916-1930," unpublished notes, provided by Sarah Koeppe.

Thomson, John, "The Land and the People of China," Society for Promoting Christian Knowledge, London, 1876.

Thomson, John, "The Chinese," Bobbs-Merrill Company, Indianapolis, Indiana, 1909

Warnshuis, Rev. A.L., M.A., "A Brief Sketch of the Life and Work of Dr. John A. Otte," Amoy Mission, China , 1911

Williamson, Rev. G.R., "Memoir of the Rev. David Abeel, D.D." Robert Carter, New York, 1848

Wright, Arnold, Editor-in-Chief, "Twentieth Century Impressions of Hongkong, Shanghai, and other Treaty Ports of China," Lloyd's Greater Britain Publishing Company, Ltd., London, 1908

Variations on Romanization of Chinese Names

Even into the 20th century, there was no standardized Romanized spelling of most Chinese names. Amoy was complicated further by the fact that place names were rendered in both Mandarin Chinese and, primarily, Amoy Dialect Romanizations.

厦门：Xiamen: Amoy, E'meng, Hsiamen, Emwy, Hemouy, Hiamen, Emowi

鼓浪屿：Gulangyu: Kulongsu, Koolangsoo, Koolangsu, Cullemshoe

泉州：Quanzhou: Chinchew, Chin-chew, Chinchu, Chwanchow, Tsuen-tcheou-foo, Chincheo, Cayton, Zaitun, Zayton, Zaiton, Zaithoum

福州：Fuzhou: Fu-cheuo-foo, Fuchow, Foochow, Fuh-Chau., Focheu

台湾：Taiwan: Teywon, Formosa

郑成功：Koxinga: Cocksing, Coxinga

福建：Fujian, Fukien, Fuh-kien, Fokyen

图书在版编目(CIP)数据

商业老厦门:现代中国商业与工商管理教育的摇篮:汉英对照/(美)潘维廉著,潘文功译. —厦门:厦门大学出版社,2012.6(2019.2重印)
(魅力·老潘)
ISBN 978-7-5615-4295-8

Ⅰ.①商… Ⅱ.①潘…②潘… Ⅲ.①商业史-史料-厦门市-汉、英 Ⅳ.①F729

中国版本图书馆 CIP 数据核字(2012)第 103725 号

出版人	郑文礼
责任编辑	施高翔

出版发行 厦门大学出版社
社　　址　厦门市软件园二期望海路 39 号
邮政编码　361008
总 编 办　0592-2182177　0592-2181406(传真)
营销中心　0592-2184458　0592-2181365
网　　址　http://www.xmupress.com
邮　　箱　xmup@xmupress.com
印　　刷　厦门集大印刷厂

开本　720 mm×1 000 mm　1/16
印张　14.5
插页　4
字数　218 千字
版次　2012 年 6 月第 1 版
印次　2019 年 2 月第 2 次印刷
定价　35.00 元

本书如有印装质量问题请直接寄承印厂调换

厦门大学出版社
微信二维码

厦门大学出版社
微博二维码